WALKING ON THE
WORD

A 40-DAY DEVOTIONAL
MOVING FROM FEAR TO FAITH

ERELETHEIA ALLEN

*A book for anyone struggling to take the leap of faith
toward the things the Lord is calling you to do.*

ELOHAI
INTERNATIONAL
PUBLISHING & MEDIA

Published by ELOHAI International Publishing & Media
P.O. Box 1883, Cypress, Texas 77410
www.elohaiintl.com

Printed in the United States of America

Library of Congress Control Number: 2025918568

Print ISBN: 979-8-9998668-9-9
Ebook ISBN: 979-8-9998668-8-2

CONTENTS

"Ereletheia Allen has definitely brought to life the saying "easier said than done" as it pertains to stepping out in faith. Her gentle and very digestible writing allows the reader to genuinely feel as though she is personally present with them on their journey to brave forward and "get out of the boat." And to know that all things are possible when God has ordained a thing.

I thoroughly enjoyed reading her 40-day devotional as it has renewed my own current summons from our Lord to get out of my present personal professional boat and walk on water again by trusting Him deeper still daily.

This devotional is a must read for anyone needing a loving nudge to trust God even more that He will be with you every step of the way but you have to get out of the boat and keep your eyes fixed on Jesus."

LaTina Dorsey MA., EdS. Crisis Counselor
Trauma Recovery Specialist
Author of *The Life of a Trauma Queen:*
My Road to Redemption

"Every page is full of Word, wisdom, and practical steps you can actually live out... She carries the oil to break down scripture in a way that challenges you, encourages you, and reminds you to walk in the authority and purpose God already gave you. If you're ready to be stirred, sharpened, and strengthened in your walk with God, get this devotional. Period."

Markita D. Collins
Bestselling Author, Speaker,
Licensed Minister, Certified Life Coach

"This devotional gives the roadmap to how we can grow in our faith and trust God to accomplish what He is calling us to do if we keep our focus on Him. If anyone desires to move into their next level of God's calling, then I highly recommend this devotional!"

Cynthia R. Moore, LGPC, ACC

Walking on the Word provided me with practical tools to locate where I am in life and intentionally apply God's Word to my present circumstances. This book offers actionable, biblical strategies for living the abundant life that God has promised, helping me align my thoughts, actions, and decisions with His truth. I found it both insightful and transformative, offering guidance that is immediately applicable to everyday life."

Dr. Andreia Searcy

"Ereletheia has provided us with a treasured tool to propel us into our Kingdom assignments. Reading through the daily devotions has encouraged me to keep my focus on Jesus and not my current challenging circumstances. This devotional certainly serves as a personal confirmation that what God has placed inside of me and what He wants to do through me is a threat to the kingdom of darkness. Therefore, my faith is stirred to keep seeking and trusting God in spite of the opposition, knowing that He will see me through to become victorious for His glory."

Shawn Hawkins

FOREWORD

The devotional *Walking on the Word* is a God-inspired devotion that is packed with an amazing amount of inspiration that involves identifying segments of scripture. I marvel at God's grace through Rev. Ereletheia Allen as she thoughtfully points us to pray and to pursue God's purpose for our lives.

This 40-day devotion is prophetic, timely, and desperately needed in our day to push our faith beyond the beyond. This will be one of the most enriching and empowering devotionals you have ever read.

Rev. Anthony R Medlock, Pastor
New Home Baptist Church
Founder And Overseer, Resurrection Life Community Church

This powerful devotional book takes us on a 40-day journey that will impact and practically unveil God's purpose for your life!

Walking on the Word guides us on a journey with the Lord that is second to none! It calls us to approach Him, love Him, to wait for Him, and most importantly to hear Him!

Rev. Ereletheia Allen gives 40 scriptural accounts and spiritual principles that show us how to posture ourselves to personally know and understand God's plan.

Today, with all the voices that seek to crowd our minds, God wants to deliver you from everything that hinders you from completing His divine fulfillment in your life. These 40 days will set your life on the trajectory God has created you for!

Rev. Joyce C. Medlock, First Lady
New Home Baptist Church

ACKNOWLEDGEMENTS

First and foremost, I thank Jesus for allowing me to fulfill what He started in me several years ago. I am so thankful that the Lord never gives up on us. I give all glory, honor and praise to God. He is the reason that I exist and without Him I can do absolutely nothing. I am so grateful for the indwelling and filling of the Holy Spirit who empowers me and encourages me even when I don't feel like I can. I love you, Lord!

Kenneth, the love of my life and very best friend, thank you for challenging me and encouraging me to walk into all that the Lord has ordained for me to walk in. Thank you for loving me unconditionally and always praying for me and praying over me. God continues to keep His promise in our lives. This is just another step in the fulfilment of what He has spoken. I love you, today, tomorrow, and forever!

To my baby girl, Jayla, I love you! I thank God for blessing me with you. You have filled my life with so much love and joy. God has used you to show me a love that goes beyond what I could have ever imagined.

To the best parents a girl could ever have, Earl, Jr. and Lillian Smith, I love you! Thank you for the loving, safe, and nurturing environment that you created for us growing up. Thank you for introducing us to Jesus. Thank you for supporting me and believing in me, regardless of how seemingly wild the idea. (LOL!) You taught me to dream and to believe that all things are possible to him that believeth.

To all my family and friends, I dare not start calling names as I don't want to forget anyone. This work isn't the result of one day or a single season, but a culmination of a lifetime of experiences, of which you were a part. Whatever the part you played in my life, I thank you, for nothing is wasted in God. Thank you for every prayer prayed for me over the years. Thank you for the encouragement and love shown to me. I love and appreciate you all! A special shout out to LaQuiesia, LaTesheia, Earvient, Tre, Kiara, Octiavia, Kynnedy, Bryce, Kayden, Avery and Ariya, I love you!

Pastor and First Lady Medlock, God placed you in my life for a time such as this and I am forever grateful for your love, encouragement, teaching, correction, and prayers! The two of you have been the blessing that I didn't even realize that I needed. Thank you for "seeing" me and pouring oil into my wounds. Most importantly, I thank God for your love for Jesus and His people. I love you both!

And lastly, thank you to ELOHAI International Publishing & Media for hearing my heart and working with me to make this work available for all to consume.

INTRODUCTION

*"And Peter answered him and said, Lord, if it be thou, bid me come
unto thee on the water. And he said, Come. And when Peter was
come down out of the ship, he walked on water to go to Jesus."*
Matthew 14:28–29 KJV

What do you do when you know that there is more or that there is a 'next' awaiting you, but there is something that keeps you from moving forward? What do you do when God is calling you to take action, but you just can't seem to take the next step? Perhaps it's fear that keeps you paralyzed, or maybe it's simply that the thought of it all seems so improbable or even downright impossible. And let's not dismiss the fact that there are times when the Lord beckons, and if we are honest, we simply don't want to go where the Lord is asking us to go. Well, wherever you may find yourself today, know that you are not alone. You are not the first person that God has asked the seemingly impossible of. While the ask He has of you may be different from the ask He has for the next person reading this, the one thing that remains true for everyone is that He never asks us to do something that He won't equip us to do. So, if He asks, He will also equip. Let's look at a Bible story to see what happened when Jesus asked a man to do the impossible.

There once was a man named Peter. He was a disciple, or follower of Jesus. Chapter 14 of Matthew tells how Jesus fed 5,000 men, plus women and children. After this, Jesus tells his disciples to get on a ship and go to the other side so that He could be alone to pray. The disciples did as they were told, but when the ship was in the middle of the sea, strong winds picked up and began to toss the ship along the waves. During the night, while the disciples' boat was being rocked by the waves, Jesus decides to take a little walk on the water.

While Jesus was walking on the water, the disciples on the boat saw him. The Scripture says they became fearful not knowing it was Him. Jesus assured the disciples that it was He and told them not to be afraid. Well Peter, wanting to know whether it really was Jesus or not, challenges Jesus and asks Jesus to tell him to come out on the water if it was really him. Jesus responds and says, "Come."

Whoa! Jesus was walking on the water and now He asks Peter to do the same. Now Peter, hearing the summons from Jesus to come to Him, got out of the boat and began to do the impossible. Peter walked on water; he walked on water to go to Jesus.

Now what's interesting about this passage is that when Jesus summoned Peter, He didn't give Peter a lesson on how gravity would be defied and how the water would be able to support him. Jesus simply said, "Come." He spoke a word; a word that was enough for Peter. At the word of Jesus, Peter got out of the boat and walked on water. There were others on the boat. There were others that saw Jesus walking on the water, but it was only Peter that did the impossible.

So, what was it exactly that allowed Peter to accomplish this miraculous feat? There were two crucial factors at work. The first was Peter's sight line. Peter's eyes were fixed on Jesus. As long as his eyes were fixed on the One that bid him to come, Peter was able to defy gravity and do the miraculous.

The second factor at work was Peter's faith in the word spoken by Jesus. Peter was on a ship in the middle of the ocean. Jesus told Peter to come to him on the water and Peter stepped out of the boat in obedience. Now, at face value, this may sound like it was foolish of Peter to jump out of the boat, but Peter had history with the Lord. He knew for a fact that the Lord only wants what's best for us. Peter knew of Jesus' miracle working power and so he knew that if the Lord said a thing, then He could also make it good. So, Peter fixed his eyes on Jesus and took Jesus at His Word. Jesus said, "Come," and Peter did just that. Peter got out of the ship to walk on the water to Jesus. Peter walked on the Word of God.

Jesus told Peter to "Come," but what has the Lord spoken to you? What is it that you sense the Lord asking you to do? Is it something seemingly impossible or improbable, like walking on water? Or is it something that seems well beyond your capabilities or even strikes a bit of fear in your heart? Whatever it is the Lord speaks and asks of you, we must recall, like Peter, that He only wants the best for us. We must, like Peter, set our sight line on Jesus and take the leap of faith and walk on the word that God has spoken to us.

Now, I know that when God is asking us to move out of our comfort zone, it's often easier said than done. If we can be honest, sometimes it's downright scary. So, I invite you to join me on a journey over the next forty days as we embark on a journey that will strengthen you and encourage you to move forward in the things that the Lord is speaking to you.

This devotional is specifically written for anyone that senses the Lord asking you to take a leap and move forward in faith. This devotional will walk you through coming into agreement and acceptance of what the Lord has called you to do. Once you have come into agreement, we will move into the action phase in which we begin taking steps toward the fulfillment of the assignment and then the devotional concludes with encouragement to continue to move forward once the initial excitement has faded and the real work to keep going has begun.

Each day of the devotional starts with a theme and focus verse for meditation. Every message concludes with an opportunity to reflect and apply the focus for the day. And lastly, each day concludes with a prayer prompt. The prayer prompt is designed to be a launching board for you to go to the Lord in prayer about that day's message.

So, whether, you are taking a first step on a new project or assignment, pursuing a God given dream, continuing in an existing assignment or making a pivot away from that which is known and comfortable, whatever the case may be, Jesus is summoning you to a place of greater faith in the word that He has spoken. He desires to accomplish something that is seemingly impossible, through you! So, if you are ready to Walk on the Word of God, let's get started.

DAY 1: IS THAT YOU LORD?

"And when he putteth forth his own sheep, he goeth before them, and the sheep follow him: for they know his voice. And a stranger will they not follow, but will flee from him: for they know not the voice of strangers."
John 10:4–5 KJV

Before we can walk on the Word of God, we must first hear that which the Lord is speaking to us. However, often in the busyness of life, we get so preoccupied with the things that we "have" to do that we don't make the time we should to sit still so that we can hear God. And many times, even when we do make the decision to sit before the Lord, we have so many other things going on in our head that when He does speak, we aren't even sure that it's Him. Perhaps this is where you are today.

The truth of the matter is our Father desires to talk to us. He longs to be able to share and reveal the plans that He has for our lives. The great news is that not only does He long to talk to us, but Scripture also assures us that we who belong to Him can hear His voice. We have the ability to know His voice and hear Him clearly.

Learning to recognize the voice of God happens in much the same way that we learn to recognize the voices of our family members and friends. We know the voice of family and friends because we are around them so much that their voice becomes familiar. The same is true with the voice of God. The more that we talk with Him, the more familiar and certain we become of His voice.

When we go to the Lord in prayer, we should approach prayer like we do a conversation with a friend. Just as we wouldn't have a conversation with a friend, do all the talking and then get up and leave, this shouldn't be our approach to conversations with Jesus, either. When we go to the Lord in prayer after we finish talking, sit for a bit and listen to what He has to say. Make note of any impressions or thoughts that come to mind as you sit. Often, the Lord will use these impressions to communicate with us. Get yourself a journal and make notes of what you sense.

The Lord also speaks through His Word. Before you read, ask the Lord to give you revelation as you read the Word. If you sense Him leading you to a particular passage of Scripture, ask Him to highlight what He wants you to see in the text. Make note of anything that stands out to you or catches your attention as you read. And take note of what you sense or comes to mind as you read. If you are unsure whether what you sense is from Him, ask Him. He loves when His children talk to Him and it's His delight to reveal Himself to them.

Reflection: Make time today to sit still in the presence of God and listen for His voice. Take some time to talk to the Father in prayer. There is no right way or wrong way to talk with Him. The key is to be honest and sincere in your prayer. Our Father is all knowing so there is no need to try to hide our true feelings. As 1 John 3:20 reminds us, the Lord knows all things including our heart. He's just waiting for us to humbly come before Him. So, take all that concerns you to Him. He loves when His children come to Him as Father. Once you have finished talking to Him, sit quietly listening for His voice. God speaks in many ways, so be open to learning the ways He speaks to you. For some, He speaks audibly, for some He may speak by way of an impression in your heart or what seems like a random thought.

For others, He may speak through visions, dreams, or even other people and things in your environment. As you sit, take note of what you "hear." For some, sitting still with God may be challenging at first. I get it, but don't give up. It may help to start by setting a timer for five minutes and just sit quietly until the timer goes off. As you become more comfortable, you can increase the time on your timer until you get to the place that you don't require a timer, but can just sit until you sense God release you. What is God saying to you?

Prayer Prompt: Dear Father, thank you that You love to speak to Your children. I thank you that not only do You speak to me, but I thank You Lord that I hear Your voice. So, Father, I open myself up to You. What is it that You would like to say to me today?

DAY 2: WRITE THE VISION

"Then the Lord answered me and said: 'Write the vision and make it
plain on tablets, That he may run who reads it. For the vision is yet for an
appointed time; But at the end it will speak, and it will not lie. Though it
tarries, wait for it; Because it will surely come, It will not tarry.'"
Habakkuk 2:2–3 NKJV

For years, whenever I thought of a vision, I thought it had to involve something grandiose or huge. Many times, visions are huge and other times the vision (that which God has spoken for you to do) may seem relatively small and simplistic, but it is in no way less significant.

According to our focus verse, the Bible tells us to write down the vision. When God speaks and gives an assignment, it is crucial that we write it down. Not that God will forget, but it's important that we write it down so that we don't forget what God has said. Too often, we are tempted to rely solely on our memory. The problem with that is our memory can be tricky. Think about it like this. When we first get the word from the Lord, it's like a picture in our mind. The picture is vivid, and the details are crisp. We can see the details in both the foreground and even the background.

But verse 3 indicates that the vision God gives us may not always manifest itself immediately. Often there is a season of time that passes between the time the vision is given and the manifestation. And during that season, there will likely be situations and circumstances that will arise that may seem to speak against the vision that God has given you. It is during those times that doubt, discouragement, and disappointment may threaten to set in. Once some time has passed, the details regarding what the Lord said can become hazy. It's like the clear, vivid details of the picture in our mind become less so. We may still be able to make out the images in the foreground, but that which was in the background can become so blurred as to make it totally illegible.

This is why writing the vision is so important. When time has elapsed and those seasons of challenge arise before the manifestation, we have to remind ourselves of the things that God has already declared shall be. The devil wants to bring discouragement so that we lose hope and give up. However, since God can not lie, we know with a certainty that if God said it, He will bring it to pass! Though the vision may take time to manifest, never lose sight of that which God has spoken because, at God's appointed time, it will manifest.

Reflection: If you haven't done so previously, take time to write out the vision that God has given you. For those who have already written out the vision, go back and reread that which you wrote to remind yourself of God's promises to you. Post the vision in a place that is visible, so you are reminded of what God has promised. When discouragement and doubt attempt to creep in, remind yourself and the devil of what God has said by declaring it into the atmosphere. Pray over the vision and ask the Lord whether there are things that He is asking you to do now in this season while moving toward the fulfillment of this vision? What steps will you take in obedience?

Prayer Prompt: Thank you, Lord, for the work that You have entrusted me to do. I know that I can do nothing without You. Lord, show me the next step that You want me to take toward fulfilling the assignment that You have asked of me.

Day 3: God Wants a Yes!

*"And I heard the voice of the Lord saying, "Whom shall I send,
and who will go for us?" Then I said, "Here I am! Send me.""*
Isaiah 6:8 ESV

When we as parents ask our children to do something, we like for them to respond with a "yes ma'am, yes sir" or some indication of compliance with that which we've asked of them. Furthermore, we expect this from them without any complaints, questions, or even excuses as to why they don't feel like or want to honor the request.

Now if we as humans expect that, imagine how much more our all-wise and sovereign Father desires us, His children, to answer Him. The difference between our Heavenly Father and us is that He will never force us to comply with His will. He will ask. He may even allow circumstances to become so uncomfortable that we feel like we are being forced, but He always gives us free will. From the beginning of time, God has always given mankind that ability to choose. So, as much as He wants the best for us, He won't make us choose His way. But it's His desire that we choose to comply with what He asks of us simply because of our love for Him.

Our Father is omniscient. He knows all. He knows what has happened and knows what will happen. He created us and He knows us better than we know ourselves. He knows what we are capable of because He knows what He's placed in us, and He knows exactly what it will take to draw out that which He has placed in us. Our Father knows all that we've been through, and He knows what's in store for our future. Not only that, but more importantly, He loves us! He loves us with an unfailing and uncompromising love. He loves us with a love that gave the best that He had for us. And by giving us His best, His only begotten Son Jesus, He has shown us that He wants only the best for us. He has shown us that there is nothing that He would withhold from us.

Who wouldn't love someone that loves them so dearly? Our Father would never request anything of us that will cause us harm. He has been knocking at the door of your heart, waiting for you to give Him a yes. It's His desire that we would trust His love for us such that we would give Him our unwavering yes. Give God your yes, not because you understand all that He is asking of you; not because it seems possible or even probable. But give the Father your yes, because you trust that He loves you so much that He will watch over and protect you, even through the uncertainty. Make today the day that you say yes to that which He is asking of you!

Reflection: Pray and ask God to reveal those areas of your life in which you have not said, "Yes." Ask the Father to show you what's holding you back from giving Him an unequivocal yes in every area of your life. Ask the Lord to help you trust His love for you, so that you can give Him a yes!

Prayer Prompt: Father, I pause in this moment to give You a renewed yes. I give You a yes to all that You are asking of me. I know You love me and have great plans for my life. As an expression of my love for You, I give you my yes!

Walking on the Word

DAY 4: COMPLETE SURRENDER

"'Father, if you are willing, please take this cup of suffering
away from me. Yet I want your will to be done, not mine.'"
Luke 22:42 NLT

Now that we've made up our minds to say yes to the things God desires for us, it's time to take it a step further—complete surrender; completely yielding your will and desires for your life to the Father. God wants a yes, but not only does He want you to trust His love for you, He desires that you come into agreement with Him concerning His plans for your life. He desires that you surrender your plans, your thoughts, your will, your heart, and your emotions. The Father wants you to surrender ALL to Him.

Total surrender can seem frightening because it means giving up control over your life and allowing the Lord to take control. It echoes the words of Jesus when He said, *"Father, if thou be willing, remove this cup from me, nevertheless, not my will, but thine be done."* Luke 22:42 (KJV)

Think back to the TV shows when the criminal who's been caught by the police finally surrenders. He comes out with his hands up, yielding and agreeing to comply with whatever instructions the police give him at that point. That's the posture that we should take when we surrender fully to the Lord. When we surrender to God, we, too, must come in a yielded posture. We, too, must come with the mindset that we are tired of trying to do it on our own. We must come with an acknowledgement that our own way isn't good enough and that our way only leads to defeat. We must come willing to follow the lead of our all-sovereign Father. We must allow Him to fully take the reins of our life, allowing Him to lead and have control of every aspect of our lives. God wants a yes, but even more than that, He desires that we live a life of surrender to Him.

Jesus, who is very much God, walked the earth as a man. As Jesus sat in the garden of Gethsemane, He was clear on the purpose for which He came to earth. However, this same Jesus, who previously proclaimed that He came to do the will of the Father, in His humanity, acknowledges that He didn't desire the suffering. But even in Jesus' acknowledgment of His desire, He also acknowledged that He wanted the will of the Father more. In this moment, Jesus illustrates what complete surrender looks like. He illustrates that when we surrender totally to the Father, we willingly lay down our desires so that God's perfect will may be done.

That's the thing about complete surrender. It doesn't mean that we will not have desires or want for things that are contrary to God's perfect will, but it does mean that you want God's will for your life more than your own will for your life. It means that you are willing to set aside your own will and desires so that the Lord's will may be done. When we surrender, what we come to know is that there is something precious about the Lord's will being done in our lives. When we surrender, we discover that when it's the Lord's will, we know that it's also a part of His plan and we have an assurance that all things are working together for good.

Reflection: Have you fully surrendered your life to the Lord? What areas are you holding back from allowing God to have full reign in your life? Ask the Holy Spirit to reveal to you what's causing you to hold back and then ask Him to help you to fully surrender in every area of your life.

Prayer Prompt: Search me, oh God, and know my heart. Father, You see me just as I am and You know everything about me. Show me Lord. Show me the areas that I am still holding on to and have not surrendered to You. Help me to let go of the desire to control my life and surrender my whole life to You.

DAY 5: THE INFALLIBLE TRUTH ABOUT GOD

"And God said unto Moses, I AM THAT I AM: and he said,
Thus shalt thou say unto the children of Israel,
I AM hath sent me unto you."
Exodus 3:14 KJV

After God appeared to Moses and assigned him the task of going to Pharaoh to demand that he let the children of Israel go, Moses asked the question, *Who shall I say to the children of Israel that has sent me?* God simply replied to Moses, "I AM THAT I AM."

God has given each of us an assignment that He has just for us to complete. If we can be honest and lay the cards on the table, God-sized assignments usually seem much more that we can handle. That's because He never meant for us to complete the assignment without Him. He's given you the assignment, but He is the One that plans to do the work through you. So, it is important as we go forward that we always remember who it is that has sent us. It's important to know that when God gives an assignment, it is I AM THAT I AM that has sent us.

Fortunately for us, when God describes himself as I AM THAT I AM, He's not just revealing to us a name, but it is a reminder of His very nature. The word 'AM' is the first person singular present tense of the word 'be' which means to exist. So, when He says to us by way of His name, I AM, He conveys to us that He is and always will be a present God. He conveys that He exists now in this very moment, every moment prior and every moment that shall be. I (God) AM. I AM all that you need. I AM all that you will ever need. I AM your Father. I AM your Savior. I AM your all sufficiency, I AM your deliverer, I AM your protector. I AM your sustainer. I AM your provider. I AM your way maker. I AM your healer. I AM the way the truth and the life. I AM the beginning and the end. I AM living water. I AM Sovereign God. I AM Omniscient. I AM the Omnipresent One. I AM THAT I AM.

Reflection: Who do you need God to be for you in this season of your life? Fill in the blank with who you need God to be for you now. I AM your _____. Pray and ask the Lord to be exactly what you need Him to be. God is still I AM THAT I AM and He longs for us to recognize that He is ALL that we ever need.

Prayer Prompt: Dear Lord, I thank you for being I AM. Thank you for being all that I have ever needed, even when I didn't even recognize that I needed it. As I reflect on my life now, I realize that I need You. Father, reveal yourself to me today and remind me that You are still I AM in every area of my need.

_____

_____

_____

_____

_____

_____

_____

_____

_____

_____

_____

_____

_____

_____

_____

_____

_____

_____

_____

_____

DAY 6: HE'S GOD... NOT MAN

"God is not a man, that he should lie; neither the son of man,
that he should repent: hath he said, and shall he not do it?
or hath he spoken, and shall he not make it good?"
Numbers 23:19 KJV

In the days that we are living in, the word of others doesn't seem to carry much weight anymore. Often people make promises and fail to follow through with the things that they have promised us. So much so that many people have conditioned themselves to not even get their hopes up when someone makes a promise to them.

This is unfortunate because we should be able to trust the promises made to us. But, although man/humankind may fail to keep their word, our God will never fail to keep His word. Our focus verse for the day reminds us that God isn't like mankind. It reminds us that while people may lie, God never will. It's not in His nature to lie. Not only that, but the Bible also tells us that He is not even capable of lying. Our God cannot lie!

Now, I want you to pause and wrap your head around that for a minute. God does not lie. He has not, nor will He ever say anything that is not true. His track record is proven. He has not, nor will He ever say anything that won't come to pass. Because of this, we have an assurance that when the Lord makes us a promise that it's a sure thing. It must come to pass.

Now that's good news because it means that every promise He's ever made is true! Every. Single. Word. His written Word is true, just as the word that He spoke to your heart is true as well. Everything that the Lord has declared over your life has to come to pass, just as He said. Knowing this is key because between every promise and its manifestation, there is a middle that often looks nothing like what was promised. So, knowing that what God has said has to come to pass gives us confidence to endure the middle. Knowing God doesn't lie provides comfort during the season in which what we see looks completely opposite of what was promised. But knowing that God's Word must manifest gives us the assurance to hold on, no matter what it looks like or how long it takes before we see the manifestation. So, take heart and know that it's not a matter of whether it will happen, it's simply a matter of when. And we know that God's timing is perfect, so when it does come to pass, it will be at the perfect time!

Reflection: How does knowing that God's Word is a sure thing change how you feel about that which God has spoken to you? Knowing that God's Word must come to pass, what Scriptures can you hold on to encourage you on your faith walk? Take some time and write those Scriptures down and post them in a place that you can see daily as a reminder to yourself of what God has said.

Prayer Prompt: Thank you, Lord, that every word that You have spoken is true! Thank you, that what You have declared about me is true, and thank you that what You have said about this assignment is true. Father, I ask today that You would help me to stand on what You have said with confidence and boldness, knowing that Your word is true!

DAY 7: THE SURETY OF GOD'S WORD

*"So shall my word be that goeth forth out of my mouth:
it shall not return unto me void, but it shall accomplish
that which I please, and it shall prosper in the thing whereto I sent it."*
Isaiah 55:11 KJV

Being assured of God's character is crucial for anyone pursuing a God-given assignment. For it is the knowledge of His character that will give you additional assurance as you step out in faith. Yesterday, we discussed the fact that God cannot lie. Today's focus verse takes it a step further. Not only does the verse confirm that His Word is true, but this verse also confirms that 1) God's Word always manifests and accomplishes what it says it will do, 2) when God sends His Word, He has an intended plan for everything that He says and 3) God's Word always aligns with His Will.

Let's examine these three points a little closer. The first thing that this verse tells us is that God's Word always manifests and accomplishes what it says it will do. If God says a thing, then it will always come to pass. As we discussed yesterday, He can't lie and because He can't lie, if He says something, it will happen. But the verse goes on and lets us know that when God sends His Word, He has an intended plan for what He has said. This is key to know that God is intentional in everything that He says. God doesn't waste words. God never misspeaks, and He doesn't just talk idly.

Secondly, our Heavenly Father has a plan for each of our lives. Before you were born, He mapped out every day of your life and created you on purpose for a specific purpose. He placed gifts and callings in you, and He uses His Word to direct you towards the fulfillment of His plan for your life. He uses His Word to reveal Himself to you and draw you into a relationship with Him so that you would yield yourself to Him and allow Him to use you to advance the kingdom of God on Earth and bring glory to Him. Even that which He is calling you to do now is a part of His plan to reveal Himself to you in an even greater way and an invitation to allow Him to use you for His glory!

Lastly, this verse assures us that His Word aligns with His will. Why is this important? First John 5:14–15 (KJV) says, *"And this is the confidence that we have in him, that, if we ask any thing according to his will, he heareth us: And if we know that he hear us, whatsoever we ask, we know that we have the petitions that we desired of him."* When we pray that which is according to God's will, we have an assurance that we shall have what we pray for. This assignment that the Lord has spoken to you and invited you to participate with Him on is a Word spoken to you from the Lord. As you pray about it and seek God's direction and strategy for how to do that which He has assigned to you, you have an assurance that in His time, the Lord will provide that which you are seeking because it is in His will for you.

If you take away nothing else from today's devotion, know that God's Word is sure. It's sure in its purpose and it's sure in its manifestation. Know that this is a part of God's plan for your life. You may not understand it or even see how this could possibly fit into His plan for your life, but our inability to understand what the Father is doing doesn't negate His sovereignty. Everything that God speaks shall come to pass!

Reflection: Reflect on God's track record in your life. Can you trace things that the Father has spoken to you before and the manifestation of those things? Think about the Word that He is speaking to you in this season. How does the knowledge that God is intentional in all that He does and that this assignment is a part of His larger plan for your life affect how you view the assignment that He has for you? How does it make you feel knowing that everything He has spoken shall come to pass?

Prayer Prompt: Father, thank you for the surety of Your Word. Admittedly, I don't always see the big picture for my life the way You do, but I thank you that You don't require me to see it for it to be true. So, Lord, I thank you now for the manifestation of what You have said. It is so and I thank you for bringing it to pass.

Day 8: He Won't Change His Mind About You

"For the gifts and the calling of God are without repentance."
Romans 11:29 KJV

I f you're anything like me, changing your mind is something that you are prone to do. In fact, you may even feel like it's your right or privilege to do so. If you feel this way, you are not alone. Most people change their minds regularly about decisions that they've made in life. Whether it's the outfit that you plan to wear for the day, the career choice, or the meal that you are planning to eat, having a change of mind is a regular occurrence.

So, it's not farfetched for us to feel that God will change His mind about the assignments that He gives us, right? Wrong! Nothing can be further from the truth. While it is commonplace for us to change our mind regarding our plans, God does not change His. He doesn't make mistakes or need to change His mind about what He has purposed.

This is even true concerning the plans that He has for your life. The plans He has for your life are not subject to your mood, your behavior, your agreement, or your approval. The Amplified Bible states Romans 11:29 like this: *For the gifts and the calling of God are irrevocable [for He does not withdraw what He has given, nor does He change His mind about those to whom He gives His grace or to whom He sends His call.]* God will not change His mind regarding His intentions or desires for you and what He has gifted and called you to do.

Israel was God's chosen people. As rebellious as they were, and even though they turned their back on God and He allowed them to suffer the consequences of their choices, He never forsook them as His chosen people. Just as with the children of Israel, our choices can also cause us to forfeit or even delay that which God has determined for us. God is not wishy-washy. He is not some-timey or moody. He is omniscient and knows the ending from the beginning, so there is no guesswork in what He declares. When He declares a thing about you and me, He already knows the end and how it will work out. Our Father always wants the best for His children and as the husbandman, He tends to the garden of our lives to ensure that we have what we need to live a life that is fruitful (John 15:1–2). God will not change His mind about you.

Reflection: Knowing that God won't change His mind regarding that which He has planned for your life, how does that make you feel regarding that which He has assigned you to do? Reflect on the fact that God's decision to gift you and call you to a certain assignment is not based on your actions or behaviors. How does this make you feel about God?

Prayer Prompt: Dear Father, what a blessing to know that You will not change Your mind about me. Help me to see me as You see me, so that I may embrace this truth with all my heart. Thank you for loving me so unconditionally.

DAY 9: RIGHT NOW FAITH

"Now faith is the substance of things hoped for,
the evidence of things not seen."
Hebrews 11:1 KJV

Faith has been defined as a belief in that which is not yet but prompts actions that look like it has already manifested. Faith is never tied to anything that already is or that is already visible. Faith is always attached to that which has not yet happened. Faith requires believing that while it has not yet manifested, one day it will manifest itself.

Faith causes one to be in action now. Faith causes one to begin the preparation for that which is to come. Faith causes you to create an environment for that which shall be, in your now. Any time you talk about faith, it is always tied to present actions for a future result.

Faith will make you look crazy to those without it. Faith will cause you to champion causes that others deem to be hopeless. Faith will cause you to go forward when all that you see around you tells you to stand still. But as our focus verse of the day reminds us, faith is an assurance of that which is hoped for. It's an assurance and knowing of what is not yet revealed to the natural senses. You can't see it yet, but you believe it. You have no evidence of it, but you know it to be true.

Hebrews 11 is often referred to as the faith chapter. It recounts the many faithful people of God who walked by faith believing to see that which they had been hoping. It recounts the men and women who had been given a promise, and based solely on the promise, they took action. They were so fully persuaded of the promise that they embraced what was promised and went to work toward the fulfillment of the promise, believing that it would one day come to pass.

Reflection: What is God telling you to do in faith? Write down what God is telling you and how you feel about what God is telling you. What are the benefits of going forward? What are the risks of not doing what God is telling you to do? As you continue to pray, ask God to strengthen your faith as you move forward. Pray also that you will walk by faith and not by sight and that your faith will continue to grow strong and not fail.

Prayer Prompt: Dear Lord, as I look at the faithful men and women who took You at Your word and acted in faith, I, too, desire to be included in this list. I know that faith is not about trusting what I see, but about trusting what You have said. So, thank you, Lord, for helping me to stand securely on what You have said. Day by day, I am moving forward with an assurance that what isn't visible now shall be, simply because You said it.

Day 10: A Faithful Shepherd

"The Lord is my shepherd; I shall not want."
Psalm 23:1 KJV

Psalm 23 begins with a bold declaration: "The Lord is my shepherd." A shepherd is one who protects the flock. The shepherd looks after the flock to ensure that no danger comes to the flock. When a sheep begins to stray, the shepherd guides the sheep back into place. The shepherd's whole job is to care for the sheep and to ensure that the sheep have everything that they need. The shepherd protects the sheep from the prowling wolves, seeking to devour the sheep. Because the shepherd provides protection, the sheep don't have to fear for their lives when the shepherd is present.

The shepherd also leads and guides. The sheep know not where to go except the shepherd lead them. As the shepherd leads the sheep, he navigates them around obstacles and anything that could potentially bring harm or danger to the sheep. He leads them to water when they are thirsty, and he leads them to shade to protect them from the heat of the day.

The psalmist boldly proclaims, *"The Lord is my shepherd"* and follows it up with, *"I shall not want."* I can imagine when David, the former shepherd boy, wrote this psalm that he reflected on how he cared for his sheep; how he protected, led, guided, and provided for them. I can imagine that he thought about all his sheep had to do was follow him, and he made sure that their every need was met. I can imagine that as he reflected, he concluded that as he was all these things for his sheep, the Lord is all that and more. If a young shepherd boy can protect, provide, lead, and guide, how much more can our loving and sovereign Father do! Just as sheep need only follow the shepherd and they will not suffer lack, as children of God, we, too, are assured that we lack nothing when we follow the Lord. Everything that we need, He shall provide. Everything that is meant for us, He will lead us to it. Every place that we are destined to go, He will guide our steps to ensure that we make it.

As you move forward in that which God is calling you to, don't fret over provision or how you are going to get there. Simply declare that the Lord is my shepherd, I shall not want. Find peace in knowing that as a shepherd totally provides for the sheep, your Father will do the same for you!

Reflection: As you think about what it is that the Father is asking you to do, does it make you anxious? Do you ever worry or wonder about provision or how will He do what He said He would do? Take some time to read Psalm 23 and meditate on the Lord as your shepherd.

Prayer prompt: Dear Lord, You are a faithful shepherd! Thank you for caring for me and taking care of all my needs. Just as sheep need only follow their shepherd, help me to keep my eyes fixed on You so that I can follow You as You lead. Father, if I go astray, I thank you in advance for lovingly leading me back to the fold under Your watchful and protective care.

DAY 11: FAITH UNLOCKS THE DOOR

"Jesus said unto him, If thou canst believe,
all things are possible to him that believeth."
Mark 9:23 KJV

Old ways won't open new doors. Faith is the key to unlocking all that God has in store for you. Your future, your "next" is tied to your ability to believe what God has already declared.

In our focus verse for today, we see Jesus' response to a father who brought his son to Jesus for deliverance. In the 'b' portion of verse 22 (KJV), the father says to Jesus, *"if thou canst do any thing, have compassion on us, and help us."* Though the father came to Jesus for healing, there was still some doubt about whether Jesus would actually be able to do it. At times, if we are honest, we, too, are like the father in this text. We may not actually verbalize it, but our actions convey that there are times that we doubt what we know about the Lord and whether He will really fulfill what He has said He will do.

What I like about this account is Jesus' response. Jesus simply declared to the man, *"All things are possible to him that believeth."* Jesus was telling the father that what the father desired wasn't tied to Jesus' ability, but rather to the father's ability to believe. In other words, if we remove all doubt, and simply believe, ALL things are possible because of our belief.

ALL things. Think about that. The word 'all' is inclusive. It leaves nothing out. All includes the big things as well as the little things.

It includes the things you've verbalized as well as those things that you have only dreamed about. All things are possible … even that very thing you are struggling with as you read this passage. Yes, even that is possible, if you believe. The question today is, do you believe?

Reflection: Answer the question whether you believe that what you have been called/assigned to do in this season will come to pass. If not, pray and ask the Lord to help your unbelief. Acknowledge your desire to move from this place of unbelief and doubt to a place of greater faith and belief so that you may be able to move forward in your assignment.

Prayer Prompt: Lord, as I come to you today, I come acknowledging that You are God who created the heavens and the earth. You are the One who created every living being and formed man from the dust of the earth. Creation alone speaks to your power. As I reflect on who You are, may I be reminded that You can do anything. So I thank you Lord that ALL things are possible with You. All things, including the assignment that You have asked of me.

DAY 12: HELP MY UNBELIEF

"And straightway the father of the child cried out,
and said with tears,
Lord, I believe; help thou mine unbelief."
Mark 9:24 KJV

Yesterday, we began looking at the account of the father that requested Jesus to deliver his son. This was the same father that requested Jesus' disciples to deliver his son, but they couldn't do it. I can just imagine the relief of the father when Jesus finally showed up. The father takes his son to Jesus and as we read yesterday, Jesus told the father that all things are possible to him that believes. But instead of the father becoming exuberant with joy, because of Jesus' affirmation that healing was possible, the latter part of verse 24 indicates the father cried out with tears, "Lord, I believe, help thou mine unbelief."

I can imagine the thoughts that ran through the father's mind. I imagine that he likely was thinking that if anybody could heal his son, it would be Jesus, as I'm sure he'd heard of all the miraculous things Jesus had done for others. But his son had been in this condition for a long time, Scripture says, since he was a child. I can imagine the father wrestling with hope that Jesus would deliver his son while yet another part of him was still unsure. I can imagine the father thinking what so many of us have at one point or another—Lord, I know you're able, but will you do it for me?

I believe many of us have had moments or even seasons in our lives in which we could identify with the father's response in this passage. Times when we have been guilty of wanting or even needing to believe God at His word, yet still having a corner in the recesses of our heart that is colored by doubt. While we know Jesus to be Savior, there are still times when doubt and uncertainty try to creep in and cause us to question, much like the father in this passage, whether God will do it for us. Some call it not getting your hopes too high in case it doesn't pan out. Others refer to it as having a "Plan B," just in case.

What we must know is that in order to truly see the fullness of that which God has for our lives, it requires that we trust and believe Him with our ALL, withholding nothing. But far too often that flesh of ours rises and plants seeds of doubt, even when we want to believe.

It's at these times that we must be real with ourselves and with God and cry out like the father and say Lord, I believe, help my unbelief. When we come to God authentically and admit our shortcomings to Him, we acknowledge our need for His sufficiency in our lives. We acknowledge that it is only through Him working in our lives that we can do that which He requires of us. When we find ourselves in a place where doubt and uncertainty have crept in, we must be bold enough to be honest with the Lord about where we are. We must then acknowledge that it's not our desire to remain in that place of unbelief. And when we do so, we will see that just as Jesus delivered the father's son, we will see Jesus do what He said He would do in our situations.

Reflection: Spend some quiet time with the Lord and confess any areas of doubt surrounding the assignment that God has given you. For every area of doubt, pray and ask the Father to help your unbelief by reassuring you with His Word. Write down that which the Lord gives you as assurance so that when those same doubts try to creep back in, you can remind yourself of what God has already spoken.

Prayer Prompt: Dear Heavenly Father, You see the inward and hidden parts of me. There is nothing that I can hide from Your all-seeing eyes. So today, Father, while I believe that nothing is too hard for You, I confess that there are times in which I wonder whether You will really work in my life. So Father, I confess I believe, but I ask that You would help my unbelief. For every area in which there is doubt in my life, Father, help me to believe.

DAY 13: I TRUST YOU LORD

"Trust in the Lord with all thine heart;
and lean not unto thine own understanding."
Proverbs 3:5 KJV

Over the last couple of days, we have been discussing the top-ic of faith and underscoring the point that faith is essential in anything that you do with the Lord. As we discussed on day nine, faith causes you to move as if you already have that which you are believing for before you actually have it. And as we saw yesterday, it is possible to believe and yet not believe all the way. It's possible to believe in your head because you intellectually know it to be true but still struggle with that knowledge taking up residence in your heart.

Our focus verse was penned by a wise man named Solomon. In his wisdom, Solomon tells us that it's not enough to know of God's trust-worthiness, but we must also embrace what we know and allow it to fill our heart. Not only are we to trust in the Lord with all our heart, he encourages us to lean not to our own understanding. He tells us not to depend on our own understanding or logic as criteria for our belief and obedience. By following Solomon's instructions, we can live in place of total trust whether our situation make sense or not.

Now, that alone is challenging for many because we are taught to use what we have learned and what we know about life to make in-formed decisions. And all of this is true. However, the key is that we can never take what we know about life and this physical realm and allow it to trump the truth of what we know about God. To get to the place of trusting God with all our heart requires us to acknowledge that what we know and can even see regarding life's situations is limited. We must be willing to abandon our limited knowledge and understanding in exchange for confidence in the fact that the Father is all-knowing and has a great plan for our lives. The greater the revelation that we have of who God is, the easier it becomes to trust Him. This is why spending time with the Father and getting to know Him is essential for this Christian journey.

The Father loves you with an unconditional and unfailing love. He wants nothing but the best for you as His child, as evidenced by Him giving you the best that He has, His only begotten Son, Jesus. Jesus came to earth wrapped in flesh and gave His life at Calvary so that you and I could be in a relationship with the Father. God loves us so much that before we were even born or even thinking about Him, He was thinking about us. Knowing that the Father loves you so much and wants nothing but the best for you; knowing that He is sovereign and knows the ending from the beginning, can you also see that anything He asks of you, He already knows how it will work out? Let this knowledge of God's love and His sovereignty compel you to declare, Lord, I trust you!

Reflection: Trust is not something that comes easily to many people. In fact, society teaches us that we shouldn't trust people easily. Well, this may be understandable as it pertains to people, but the Lord is not like man. Make time today to search the Scripture, making notes as you read about the Father's attributes. As an example, Psalm 145:8 (KJV) states, *"The Lord is gracious, and full of compassion; slow to anger, and of great mercy."* This verse lets us know that our Father is gracious, compassionate and merciful. After reading and making notes, reflect on the knowledge of who the Father is. What characteristics about Him stand out to you the most? How does the revelation of who the Father is help you to trust Him all the more?

Prayer prompt: Thank you, Father, for giving me an even greater revelation of who You are. Thank you, Lord, that You desire only the best for me. I declare, Lord, that I trust You with all of my heart and I don't lean on my understanding.

DAY 14: BELIEVE AND RECEIVE

"And blessed is she that believed: for there shall be a performance
of those things which were told her from the Lord."
Luke 1:45 KJV

The Lord's ability to perform the miraculous in our lives is directly tied to our ability to believe God. Today's focus verse are the words of Elizabeth, who was pregnant with John the Baptist, as she spoke to her cousin Mary who had come to visit her. When Mary greeted Elizabeth, the Bible says that her baby leaped for joy in her womb as she made the proclamation of blessing over her cousin.

Now previously, the angel Gabriel had visited Mary and told her that though she was a virgin, she would give birth to a son and call him Jesus. Naturally, Mary had questions as to how she could possibly conceive, seeing as though she was a virgin. But Gabriel explained that the conception would be done by God. The angel told her that the Holy Ghost would come upon her.

Upon hearing this, Mary didn't have a lengthy conversation with Gabriel asking who, what, when, and why. Instead, Scripture records her response as unwavering acceptance: *"… be it unto me according to thy word…"* (Luke 1:38 KJV). In other words, Mary didn't ask for the details; she simply replied in agreement. She believed and accepted what was spoken to her by the angel.

This type of response is what the Lord is looking for from us. When He speaks to us, He desires that we take Him at His word. Though our circumstances may not support that which He's said, and even if our minds can't comprehend the feasibility of what was said, He still desires that we believe and thereby position ourselves to receive it.

Elizabeth proclaimed both a blessing and a prophetic declaration over her cousin, and today I proclaim and declare the same blessing and declaration over your life. Blessed are you that believed what the Lord has spoken, and I declare that there will be a performance of the things that were told to you from the Lord!

Reflection: After Elizabeth proclaimed the blessing and declaration over Mary, the Bible said that Mary praised the Lord. Take some time and praise the Lord for that which He has spoken over your life. Thank the Lord that you believe Him and the evidence of your belief is your obedience. Praise God for His faithfulness. Praise Him for just being God.

Prayer prompt: Father, I bless Your name! I magnify Your righteous and Holy Name! Father, I thank you for trusting me with what You have asked of me. Thank you, Lord, for increasing my faith to trust You enough to move in obedience. I praise you, Lord! In Jesus' wonderful name! Amen.

Day 15: Exceedingly Abundantly

*"Now unto him that is able to do exceeding abundantly above all
that we ask or think, according to the power that worketh in us."*
Ephesians 3:20 KJV

Is there anything too hard for God? I think you would agree that
there is nothing too difficult for our Father. We've read the accounts in the Bible of how God is able to do the miraculous. We
know the Scripture that tells us that nothing is impossible with God
(Luke 1:37). We've even seen God move in the midst of our lives and
those whom we love. We have history with God, and we know His
track record is proven, so we know whatever we ask of God, He is
able to do.

But our verse today reminds us that God is able to do even more than
that! Not only can He do what we need, the verse tells us that He is
able to do abundantly more and then He is able to exceed even that!
Our Father can do more than we've ever imagined! The question is,
where is our faith level? His ability to do the miraculous in our lives
is connected to our ability to believe that He will. His ability to do
exceeding abundantly is connected to the power that works in us.
What is that power? Our faith!

In the book of Mark, we see where Jesus travels from town to town,
performing many miracles. He heals the sick, delivers the demoniac,
restores withered limbs, and calms the sea. You name it, Jesus did
it. After all of this, Mark chapter 6 starts with Jesus returning to his
hometown. Jesus, who has previously healed and delivered so many,

didn't do many mighty miracles in His hometown. As a matter of fact, the Bible tells us in Mark 6:5–6, that while He was there, He didn't do many miracles because of the people's unbelief. Though Jesus is all-powerful and there is nothing too hard for Him, the people's inability to believe Him for the miraculous prevented Him from performing the very miracles that they needed.

Wow! Imagine having the miracle worker in your presence but not receiving the miracle simply because you didn't believe for it. You have worked too hard and come too far to stop now. God wants to blow your mind and do more than you thought was even possible. Stretch your faith today to believe God for exceeding abundantly more! Move in radical obedience to all that He is asking of you and watch the Lord do more than you ever thought or imagined.

Reflection: What do you need God to do? Do you believe that God is able to do it? More to the point, do you believe that He will or are you hindering Jesus from doing the miracles that you need in your life due to unbelief? Have a heart to heart with the Father and allow Him to stretch your faith to new levels.

Prayer prompt: Father, You have been continuously growing my faith to believe and trust You more. I know that this journey is a journey from faith to faith. Father, stretch my faith to trust You even more. I am ready to believe You for "exceedingly abundantly."

DAY 16: I WILL DO IT!

"Then he answered and spake unto me, saying, This is the word of
the Lord unto Zerubbabel, saying, Not by might, nor by power,
but by my spirit, saith the Lord of hosts."
Zechariah 4:6 KJV

Know this for sure, the assignment God has assigned for you to do is too big for you to do alone. The assignment is greater than your ability. You cannot complete your assignment on your own. Which is exactly why the Lord says, "I will do it!"

Too often, when God begins to reveal to us the things that He has for us to do, we become fearful because of the magnitude of the task. We quickly begin to think of all of the reasons that we will not be able to fulfill the assignment, and we begin to shy away from the task that the Father has for us.

The beautiful thing about when God enlists us is that He never intended that we fulfill the assignment on our own. Truly the only way that we will ever be able to do that which God has for us to do is through Him. It is only when God works through us that we can be successful in that which He assigns our hands to do.

So instead of approaching our assignments with a list of reasons we are not qualified for the task, let us instead approach our assignments with a list of all of God's qualifications to bring it to pass. The truth of the matter is that God is really just enlisting us to work in partnership with Him. For it is not our strength, our intellect, or our skills that will ever accomplish a God assignment. Instead, whether a big task or small, it is His Spirit that works through us to accomplish what otherwise would be impossible.

Reflection: Revisit the notes you made of the Father's attributes on Day 13. Take time and focus on those attributes. Remind yourself of just how qualified God is to work in and through you. Remind yourself that you haven't been chosen because of your ability, but rather because of God's ability to work through you.

Prayer prompt: Lord, I humble myself before You. I repent for putting more focus on me and my ability over Your ability to work through me. Forgive me for allowing fear and my perceived shortcomings to disqualify me from what You desire to accomplish through me. I acknowledge You Lord as Sovereign Father. It is You who has all power. So, Lord, I yield myself to You and avail myself to You to allow Your Holy Spirit to accomplish that which You desire to do in me and through me.

Day 17: A New Thing

"Remember ye not the former things, neither consider the things of old.
Behold, I will do a new thing; now it shall spring forth;
shall ye not know it? I will even make a way in the wilderness,
and rivers in the desert."
Isaiah 43:18–19 KJV

I often tell people that your past does not define, nor even dictate, what God can do in your future. Imagine that. What you have seen and/or experienced thus far is not even an indicator of what God is capable of doing in your life.

In fact, God is declaring that He wants to do a new thing in your life. Now is the time. Now is the season. But this new season requires that you let go of the past season to embrace what God desires to do in this season. It can be tempting to reflect on what you have seen God do and think that is the way He will move in the future. However, when we do this, we put our infinite God in a finite box.

This is the lesson that God teaches the children of Israel in our focus verse of the day. In verse 17 of Isaiah 43, the Lord recounts how He fought on their behalf against the Egyptian army at the Red Sea, drowning Pharaoh and his mighty army. He then tells them in verses 18–19, what they saw Him do back then was great, but forget that because what He did back then pales in comparison to what He is about to do now. He tells the children of Israel that He is about to do something new. As a matter of fact, He says that He is already doing it. He tells them that what He is doing is contrary to conventional wisdom and logic. He says He's making a way in places that are known for not having a path and He is causing life-giving rivers to flow in arid and barren places. What He is doing now will defy what you have known.

Stop dwelling on yesterday and past wins and losses. Yes, you've had some wins, and you've seen God move on your behalf before. You've also had some losses and disappointments. Stop waiting on God to move like He did the last time. Stop dwelling on all that hasn't worked previously. Stop dwelling on your past mistakes and short-comings. The Lord has declared that now He will do a new thing, and He is inviting you into a new season.

The doors that have been shut will be opened. Opportunities and pathways that have been blocked shall now be made available to you. God declares that what has been barren and dead in your life will now spring forth with new life. What God is doing in this season will not look like how He's done it in the past! So, don't allow the burdens of yesterday to prevent you from embracing the promise of today. Learn from your past, but do not let it dictate your future. God is limitless, and He is not bound by what you have seen Him do before.

Reflection: Take a moment to reflect. Are there things in your past that are holding you back and hindering you from moving forward in your next season? Release your fears, doubts, hurt, shame, and disappointments to the Father. Invite Him in and allow Him to re-place the hurt and disappointment of your past with the peace of His promises for your present. As you pray, release all expectations of how you thought God would do it, and allow the promise of a new thing to resonate in your heart.

Prayer prompt: Thank you, Father, that You have promised to never leave me nor forsake me and I thank you, Lord, for the promise of a new thing. Father, I lay down my disappointments from past experiences that didn't pan out the way that I'd hoped. I also lay down my expectations of how You will move in my life. I invite Your healing and comfort as I take hold of Your promise of a new thing.

Day 18: The Charge and the Promise

"And the LORD, he it is that doth go before thee; he will be with thee,
he will not fail thee, neither forsake thee: fear not, neither be dismayed."
Deuteronomy 31:8 KJV

Often when embracing the unknown, there is an element of fear or doubt that threatens to creep in. Will I be able to do it? Will my offering be received? Am I qualified to do it? Lord, is this really what you want me to do? It's normal to have thoughts such as these cross your mind as you embark on new adventures, but it's dangerous to allow these types of thoughts to linger.

As Moses was preparing for his death, He passed the baton to Joshua and charged him to lead the children of Israel to the Promised Land. I can imagine as Moses charged Joshua, that he reflected back on the feelings of inadequacy and unreadiness that he initially felt when God commissioned him to confront Pharaoh and lead His people out of Egyptian captivity. I can imagine that Moses reflected on his insecurities about his speech and the doubts that he had regarding whether the children of Israel or even Pharaoh would listen to him. I can imagine all that he went through crossed his mind along with the reminder that God was faithful through it all! I can imagine that while Moses contemplated the journey that the Lord took him on, that he concluded that no matter the obstacle or opposition, God always came through.

So, as Moses charges his successor, Joshua, he speaks from his experience and tells Joshua what he knows to be true based on his history with God. Moses tells Joshua that as he goes forward, it is the Lord that will go in front of him. He tells Joshua God will always be with him and that God will never fail Him. There is no need to fear. There is no need to feel dismayed.

And so today, I charge and encourage you with the words that Moses spoke to Joshua centuries before. While the times have changed and the task before you may be different than that of Joshua, the God of whom Moses spoke has not changed. His attributes are the same as they were back then. What Moses learned to be true of God is still true today. As you go forward, know that it is your Heavenly Father, the Almighty God, who goes before you. Psalm 139:5 (NLT) states, *"You go before me and follow me. You place your hand of blessing on my head."* This reminds us that not only does the Lord go before us, but He also has our back. Just as He was with Moses and Joshua, He shall also be with you. He will never leave you. He will never fail you. He will never forsake you, so there is no need to fear or be dismayed!

Reflection: When Moses died, Joshua took up the mantle and continued forward in all that he was charged to do. Will you take the charge and move forward in the assignment that the Lord is calling you to with the promise that God is not just sending you into the wild? He is calling you to an assignment, but it is He that goes before you and He promises never to forsake or fail you. What does it mean to you to know that the Father has gone before you, has your back and He promises not to forsake nor fail you?

Prayer prompt: Father, I have heard what it is that You are calling me to do. Thank you for going before me and having my back. Thank you for Your promise to never forsake nor fail me. I shall not fear what lies ahead because I am assured that You are with me.

Day 19: Arise, Go

"Moses my servant is dead; now therefore arise, go over this Jordan,
thou, and all this people, unto the land which I do give to them,
even to the children of Israel."
Joshua 1:2 KJV

Joel Arthur Barker, an American futurist, once said, "Vision without action is merely a daydream."[1] The same holds true with our desire for God to move in our lives. For there to be fulfillment, there first must be action on our part. We must hear what God is saying to us, then we must arise and go after that which He is calling us to do.

Yesterday, we looked at the charge that Moses gave Joshua as he was preparing to transition. After Moses' death, God spoke to Joshua and commissioned him by telling him to arise and go over the Jordan River to get to the promise. The Lord was telling Joshua that to see fulfillment, he had to first get up from his current place and secondly, he had to take action. He told Joshua that he must pursue and go after the promise. The promise is sure, but it required action from Joshua to obtain it.

The same is true with what the Lord is calling you to do. The promise is sure, but there is action required by you to obtain it. So, I say to you today, "Arise, go!" Get up from where you are today. Step into the position that God has called you to embrace for the assignment. Arise from a posture of inactivity. Arise mentally from a place

---

1 *The Power of Vision*, 1991.

of doubt and uncertainty to a posture of faith and confidence in the One who called you. Arise, go! Take action and move forward in pursuit of the promise.

Now, know that God makes no guarantee that the pursuit of the promise will be easy. As a matter of fact, He told Joshua that in order to get to his promise, Joshua would have to cross the river standing between him and his promise. I don't know what obstacles are standing between you and your promise today, but I say arise and go over, around, or even through them to get to your promise.

God is faithful to do all that He says, but He usually doesn't give us a timetable for fulfillment, only the promise that fulfillment will come. Purpose today to take action toward the fulfillment of your assignment or dream that God has commissioned and assigned for you to fulfill. Arise, Go!

Reflection: What obstacles are facing you or have faced you as you pursue your promise? Have you let the obstacles stall you or are you continuing to press forward? For any obstacle that has caused you to become stalled, take time to ask the Lord for the strategy to overcome the obstacle.

Prayer prompt: Father, You are the One that has commissioned me for the assignment, and You are the One that will cause it to be completed. Grace me with the ability to conquer every obstacle that comes before me as I draw strength, wisdom, and strategy for the journey from You.

DAY 20: PURSUE GOD'S PRESENCE

"And they commanded the people, saying, When ye see the
ark of the covenant of the LORD your God, and the priests the Levites
bearing it, then ye shall remove from your place, and go after it."
Joshua 3:3 KJV

Once we have resolved within ourselves that God's promise is sure and we finally make up our minds to go after the promise, it is then that we are likely to run into the obstacles that separate us from the promise. If you're anything like me, it is at these times that I can't help but to wonder, *Lord, how am I ever going to get past this?*

The children of Israel found themselves facing this very issue in the book of Joshua. Joshua had been commissioned by God, and he set off to lead the people to the Promised Land. As they were on their way, they found themselves at the edge of a raging Jordan River, which stood between them and their promise. With no boats or other mode of water transportation in sight, they knew that to get to God's promise, they needed to cross that river. What made matters worse was not only did they have to cross the Jordan, but they needed to cross the river at a time when the banks of the river were overflowing.

Well, after camping at the brink of the river for three days, Scripture says that the Israelite officers rose up and gave very explicit instructions to the people regarding how they were to move forward. As we look at our focus verse for today, we see that we, too, can take note and apply what the Israelite officers told them. In Joshua 3:3, the leadership tells the people that when they see the ark of the covenant of the Lord (which represents God's presence) being carried by the priests, they were to get up and go after it.

The children of Israel were on their way to lay hold of God's promise. They were at the edge of the river that separated them from their promise, and the instructions from the leadership were to go after it... not the promise, but they were to go after God's presence. They were told to move only when they saw the ark of the covenant of God move before them. It's important that we don't ever get so zealous in pursuit of the promise that we run ahead of God.

More importantly, we must never lose sight of the fact that, in order to obtain the promise, we must pursue the promise giver. When we pursue God's presence, He will lead us to the promise. As we pursue God's presence, we will not have to worry about how to get around the obstacles and opposition because we have assurance that wherever He is, provision is there also. When we take our eyes off of the promise and make Him the object of our pursuit, He will lead us exactly where He wants us to go. Matthew 6:33 (KJV) states, *"Seek ye first the kingdom of God, and his righteousness; and all these things shall be added unto you."* As we pursue His presence, we have an assurance that we have everything that is needed to lay hold of His promise.

Reflection: Have you gotten consumed with trying to figure out how the promise is going to manifest? Have you gotten so zealous in pursuing the promise that you have neglected the promise giver? If so, take time today to release your pursuit of the promise and refocus your time and energy on pursuing God's presence.

Prayer prompt: Father, forgive me for getting so caught up in the pursuit of the promise, that I prioritized the promise over You. Today I refocus and set my heart, mind, and sight on You. Thank you for being the lover of my soul. I bless You because You are God. I bless You because You are Holy and there is no one like You! Thank you, Lord, for the reminder today to pursue You and Your presence over everything!

DAY 21: STRONGER IN THE LORD

"Finally, my brethren, be strong in the Lord,
and in the power of his might."
Ephesians 6:10 KJV

When God created each of us, He created us with purpose. He has a specific plan and assignment for each of us. God knows this, but the enemy knows this as well. This is why the devil works overtime to prevent you from embracing your purpose and walking in it.

You must know that you have a very real adversary whose desire is to trip you up, frustrate you, and keep you stalled to prevent you from doing the very things that God has called you to do. John 10:10a (*NLT*) confirms this and tells us that *"the thief's purpose is to steal, kill and destroy."* Fear, doubt, distractions, obstacles, and haters are just some of the many tools that the enemy will use to keep you from moving forward. This is why it's imperative that we learn to recognize the tricks of the enemy for what they are and how to counter his plots.

As Paul prepares to close out the book of Ephesians, he concludes with a final word on spiritual warfare and how to resist the tricks of the enemy. *"Finally, my brethren, be strong in the Lord and in the power of his might"* (Eph. 6:10 KJV). I love this verse because it reminds us that we have a responsibility to allow the Lord to strengthen us. In this verse, Paul doesn't speak to our ability, instead, Paul addresses God's ability. He tells us to be strong in the Lord. Our ability to withstand the attacks of the enemy is directly proportional to the depth of our relationship with the Lord. This is another reason why it is so critical that we make spending time with the Father in prayer, reading the Word, and devotion, or private worship, a regular part of our lifestyle. The stronger we grow in our relationship with the Lord, and the more we rely on the Lord's might to empower us, the greater our ability to be successful in withstanding the plots of the enemy.

God has a great work for you, but know that the greater the work, the greater the opposition. Our Father knew that we would have opposition. This didn't take Him by surprise. The great news is that God has already given us everything that we need to overcome the opposition. We must simply use what He has given us and apply it. Resolve today to become stronger in the Lord, so that the enemy's plans won't derail you and hinder you from doing all that the Father has purposed you to do!

Reflection: In what ways can you grow in your relationship with the Lord? What are some practical steps that you can take today to begin growing even stronger in your relationship with the Lord?

Prayer prompt: Father, thank you for giving us all that we need to be successful and resist the tricks of the devil. I recognize that my strength to be able to stand and withstand comes only from You. Help me, Father, to stay connected to You so that I may grow stronger in You with each passing day.

DAY 22: ENDURING THE PROCESS

*"For you have need of endurance, so that when you have done
the will of God you may receive what is promised."*
Hebrews 10:36 ESV

As much as we would like our journey to the fulfillment of God's promise to be easy, it usually isn't. There will be twists and turns along the way. There may even be situations that rise up that may cause you to want to abandon this journey altogether. As much as we wish it were not so, we must understand that there is a process associated with every promise. And just as God has purpose in the promise, there is also purpose in the process.

One of the purposes of every process is to teach us to be joyful and content as we endure and wait on God's timing. We must learn to persevere through the good and the bad. Often there are things in us that still need to be developed so that we are able to handle fulfillment of the process. So, God will allow the detours to come on our journey so that He can develop those necessary character traits that will be required once we walk into the promise. Sometimes, He will use the process to grow and strengthen our faith. Sometimes, He will allow us to have experiences so we can become more empathetic and better positioned to meet the needs of those we will serve in the promised place. Other times, He will allow detours and delays to come so that He can reveal Himself to us in a new way. And then there are times that the Father simply wants to put us on display to be a witness for Him.

As you journey through the process towards the promise, resist the urge to get frustrated or become impatient when setbacks and detours arise. Resist the urge to run ahead of God and try to force things to happen. Instead, recall that the Father is intentional in everything, so if He allows it, there must be a reason for it. With that perspective in mind, learn to ask the Father to show you what it is that He wants you to learn through the process. Be patient, wait on Him and determine in your heart and mind to endure the process. Though it may seem tedious at times, trust that God is working even when we can't see it. The Lord's thoughts are not our thoughts, nor are His ways our ways. So, though He may not bring it to pass in the way that you thought it would manifest, trust that through the process He is building you and equipping you for that which He has promised.

Reflection: Have you experienced times in which the process seemed too much to bear? Ask God to show you what it is that He would have you to learn in the midst of your process. Take time to read about those in the Bible who endured a process before walking into their promise. Some examples include Abraham who waited over 15 years for the promised birth of his heir, Isaac (Genesis 15-21). Joseph endured thirteen years of trials and testing before seeing the manifestation of his dream (Gen 37-41). The children of Israel wandered in the wilderness 40 years after leaving Egypt to reach their promise (Exodus 15-Johsua 5). What can you take away and glean from their process that will help you to endure the process that the Lord is taking you through?

Prayer prompt: Great is the Lord and greatly to be praised! You are God and beside You there is no other. Thank you, Lord, that You are the all-wise God. You don't need to consult or take counsel from anyone, because all wisdom belongs to You. So, knowing this, Father,

I thank you. Even though I may not understand why You are taking me through this process, I trust You and acknowledge that Your ways are perfect. As I submit to Your leading, show me what it is that You would have me to learn through this process and help me to endure.

DAY 23: YOU ARE NOT ALONE

"I will not leave you comfortless: I will come to you."
John 14:18 KJV

As a child, when I was nervous about doing a task, I always wanted someone to come with me. It didn't matter if it was an adult, a sibling, or a friend. Just knowing that there was someone else to assist me made it a little easier to do that which I was apprehensive about.

Knowing that there is a great work for us to do, when Jesus was preparing to leave and return to the Father, He told His disciples that He wouldn't leave them without help. Jesus promised the disciples that He would not leave them comfortless. He promised that He would send the Comforter, who is the Holy Spirit. And true to His word, on the day of Pentecost, the Lord poured out His Spirit upon the people. He sent the Holy Spirit to aid, guide, and provide divine strength just as He said He would.

Even all these years later, the same promise that Jesus gave His disciples is true for you and me today. We are not on this journey alone. As believers, once we accepted Jesus Christ as Savior, the Holy Spirit took up residence within us. The Holy Spirit, who is 100% God, lives within us to lead us and guide us. He comforts us and enables us. He brings all things to our remembrance and empowers us with power from on high.

There is confidence in knowing that as we live day by day, we don't face the day alone. We don't encounter the trials and pressures of life alone. The Holy Spirit, who is fully God, is with us every step of the way. As you continue to move forward in faith, take comfort in knowing that you are not alone. Be comforted by knowing that the Holy Spirit is always present with you. In John 16:13, Jesus describes the Holy Spirit as the Spirit of Truth because He is the one that will guide you into all truth. In that same verse, Jesus goes on to say that the Holy Spirit only says what He hears. When the Holy Spirit speaks, you and I can be assured that what He reveals to us is true and comes from the heart of the Father.

Use this journey as an opportunity to lean into the Holy Spirit even more. It has never been the Father's intention that we would walk aimlessly through this life, haphazardly hoping that we were going in the right direction. No. Just as the disciples looked to Jesus for direction and guidance while He walked with them, the Father sent us the Holy Spirit so that we would look to the Holy Spirit and rely on Him just as the disciples relied on Jesus. Just as Jesus simply told the disciples to follow Him, we, too, are to follow the Holy Spirit as He leads. You have a helper who is always present. Allow Him to take the lead and guide you as you continue toward your God ordained destiny.

Reflection: Are there times in your life that you feel alone? Take time today to sit quietly and ask the Holy Spirit to reveal Himself to you. Be intentional about becoming conscious daily of the Holy Spirit's presence within you. Consult Him for direction and guidance and move as He instructs.

Prayer prompt: Thank you, Lord, that I am never alone. Thank you for the gift of Your blessed Holy Spirit who lives inside of me. Holy Spirit, today I yield to You. Forgive me for trying to figure life out on my own. I yield to Your leading and guidance. Show me the next step that You would have me to take and thank you for empowering me to do all that You lead me to do.

DAY 24: EVERYTHING ISN'T FOR EVERYBODY

"And I arose in the night, I and some few men with me;
neither told I any man what my God had put in my heart to do
at Jerusalem: neither was there any beast with me,
save the beast that I rode upon."
Nehemiah 2:12 KJV

Some things God reveals to you are just for you! We must know that there is a time for everything, including a time to keep things between you and the Lord. Though you may be filled with zeal and passion regarding that which God is revealing and leading you to do, you must know that it doesn't necessarily mean it's for you to reveal and share with everyone, yet.

In the book of Nehemiah, the Lord burdened Nehemiah with the task of rebuilding the wall of Jerusalem. At that time, Nehemiah was serving as the cupbearer to the king. With the blessing of both God and the king, he left his position in the Persian palace to travel to Jerusalem to take on the task of rebuilding the wall. When Nehemiah arrived in Jerusalem, he didn't come announcing what God had laid on his heart. He kept it to himself until it was the appointed time to share.

This is a valuable lesson that we must learn to adopt as we go about fulfilling that which God calls us to do. Though we may be tempted to share the things God reveals to us, it is prudent that we seek the Lord regarding who we are to share with, the appropriate time to share, and even how much or how little we are to share.

Fulfilling a God-given assignment means doing it God's way. This means that we must remain sensitive to the leading of the Holy Spirit. Our Father is omniscient, and He sees the full path to fulfillment. He knows those in your circle who have the faith to believe and partner with you for the promise, and He also knows the ones whose faith is not as strong and would speak words that may plant seeds of doubt in your heart. The Lord also knows those who are on assignment to oppose and hinder the manifestation of the promise that He has assigned for you to complete.

For Nehemiah, opposition came in the form of two men, Sanballat and Tobiah. Just like Nehemiah, you, too, will have haters assigned to you whose sole mission is to gather intel about your assignment so they can use it to try to sabotage your efforts. Despite his haters, Nehemiah completed his assignment. Moving and speaking as the Lord leads helps you to stay in the Father's will and under His protection so that you, too, can complete your assignment.

Reflection: Ask the Lord to reveal to you those you are to share the dream, vision, or assignment that He has given you. Ask Him to reveal the timing and even what to disclose. As you pray, ask the Lord to help you to temper your zeal and enthusiasm so that you don't move ahead of Him and that you will continue to move according to His will and divine timing.

Prayer prompt: Dear Father, thank you for entrusting me with this assignment. Now Father, I ask that You would reveal to me those with whom I am to share. Show me, Lord, those who will partner with me in faith toward the fulfillment of the assignment. Thank you, Lord, that I am not led by feelings, zeal, or excitement. Thank you, Lord, that I am only led by You. Help me to be discerning as I continue on this journey and may I trust everything You reveal over what I feel.

_____

_____

_____

_____

_____

_____

_____

_____

_____

_____

_____

_____

_____

_____

_____

_____

_____

_____

_____

_____

_____

_____

_____

DAY 25: DIVINE PROTECTION

"No weapon that is formed against thee shall prosper;
and every tongue that shall rise against thee in judgment
thou shalt condemn. This is the heritage of the servants of the Lord,
and their righteousness is of me, saith the Lord."
Isaiah 54:17 KJV

Every God-given assignment will face some form of opposition. Know that this is a fact! Your assignment, my assignment, and every God-given assignment ever given to man in history has faced opposition. Why? Because every God-given assignment ultimately brings glory to the Father and the devil will do whatever he can to prevent that. As a child of God, you are an enemy of Satan. He hates you and he hates the work of your hands that brings glory to the Father. He knows that He can't stop what God has planned for your life, so he brings in opposition and goes about doing things to hinder and frustrate you, with the hopes that you will abort what God has assigned you to do. Be reminded that the devil is no match for God.

Opposition can come from known enemies and even sometimes from those closest to you. It can come in many forms. Sometimes it's subtle and comes in the form of doubters and those who question whether you can do it. And other times, opposition is more blatant and comes by way of those who go to extreme lengths to hinder you and prevent you from completing your assignment.

In the previous devotion, we spoke briefly of Sanballat and Tobiah's blatant efforts to thwart Nehemiah's God-given assignment to rebuild the wall of Jerusalem. Though every attempt was made by the enemy to discourage Nehemiah, he continued to pray and trust the Lord to protect him. Now it's key to note, the Lord never stopped his enemies from plotting, nor did He prevent the 'weapons' against Nehemiah from being formed. God simply made it such that He protected Nehemiah from every plot and ensured that even though the weapons were indeed formed, their intended result wouldn't manifest. God ensured that no weapon formed against Nehemiah prospered!

Nehemiah had the favor of God on him and his assignment, but he also had haters who plotted, planned, threatened, and lied about him. When opposition and haters arise, that is not the time to begin to question whether your assignment is truly from God. Sadly, many people have erroneously taught that when you have favor with God, there will be no opposition. The truth is, more often than not, it's the exact opposite. The favor of God on your life doesn't prevent opposition. It simply means that no matter the opposition, God will cause you to prevail. Have you ever considered that just maybe the Lord allows opposition to come against those who He has favored just so that He can prove Himself strong to His favored and all those watching?

The Lord has promised that no weapons formed against you will prosper. Just as the Lord protected Nehemiah while on his assignment, the Lord will protect you too. When opposition comes, elevate your sight line; take your eyes off the opposition, and keep them fixed on Jesus. Pray and look to the Lord. Seek the Lord's counsel and protection and allow Him to fight for you!

Reflection: Have you encountered any haters on your journey? How have you handled them? Ask the Lord to help you to handle your haters in a Godly manner. Ask the Lord to prepare you for any opposition that may arise by helping you remain focused on Him.

Prayer prompt: Father, you are my protector; my help in my time of need, and for that I say thank you. Thank you, Father, that no weapon formed against me shall ever prosper. So, Father, I stand confidently and boldly in You, knowing that whatever shall come my way, You will protect me and cause me to prevail.

DAY 26: SUIT UP

"Put on the full armor of God,
so that you can take your stand against the devil's schemes."
Ephesians 6:11 NIV

Spiritual warfare is real! When you accepted Jesus Christ, you enlisted in a war, whether you knew it or not. Recall, as we discussed yesterday, the enemy hates you. He hates your Father, and he hates you because you are His child. Satan is not God's equal, so he knows that he is no match for God directly. So, instead of going after the Father, he goes after the Father's prized possession—His children. It's the devil's desire to keep us from walking in and experiencing all that the Lord has for us. He desires to abort our purpose and keep us living beneath our privilege as God's children. Not because he cares about you or your assignment, but he knows the impact that we will have in advancing the kingdom of God on Earth when we walk in obedience and unity with the Father.

Make no mistake about it. While the devil is no match for the Father, he is organized and strategic in his operation against God's creation. Just as the Father has a heavenly kingdom, the devil has a demonic kingdom. He is an imitator and copies the things of God and distorts them for his evil uses. He uses his demonic kingdom of darkness to attack and accuse God's creation to keep us bound and walking in disobedience to the Father. He lies and distorts the truth in hopes that we will buy into his lies over the truth of God's word.

But the Lord knew this would be, so He equipped us with instructions throughout Scripture on how to fight this spiritual battle. As our focus verse highlights, we are told to suit up for the battle because rest assured the devil will bring the battle to you. We are told to put on the full armor of God so that we can stand firm against the tricks and plots of the devil.

According to Ephesians 6:14–18, there is a process to putting on the armor. The first piece of armor is truth. We are to "gird our loins with truth." Truth is absolute and anything that contradicts it is a lie. The Word of God is truth and it anchors the other pieces of the armor. It also provides strength for the battle. Anything that doesn't align with the Word is a lie. Next, we are to put on the breastplate of righteousness. Righteousness is to be right with God. The breastplate covers the heart, protecting it so that it remains in a posture that is right with God. We are then instructed to put the gospel of peace on our feet. Our feet ground us and enable us to stand. The gospel of peace brings about a oneness with the Lord that allows us to stand securely regardless of the opposition.

The next piece of armor that we must put on is the shield of faith to quench the fiery darts of the enemy. Shields cover and protect so that the weapons sent are not effective in causing harm. Faith protects us in a similar manner. Our faith in God and His Word quenches the lies of the enemy and causes his attack to become ineffective. We are also instructed to put on the helmet of salvation. The primary place that the enemy likes to attack is our mind. When we put on the helmet of salvation, we are reminded of what Jesus did for us at Calvary. Our thoughts reflect the freeing truth of our Father's great love for us.

As we suit up, we continue by taking the sword of the Spirit, which is the Word of God. The Word is not just a defensive weapon; it is an offensive weapon as well. The Word of God is truth and shuts down every lie of the enemy. Lastly, we are instructed to pray. We are to remain in a posture of constant communication with our Father. Each day, make sure that you put on your full armor. When we are suited up daily, we are ensured that we have everything that we need to stand and withstand the attacks of the enemy.

Reflection: Suiting up daily must be a deliberate practice. Take a moment and reflect on your life. Are you intentional about putting on the whole armor of God? Do you suit up daily or on occasion? How can you become more intentional about ensuring that each day you dress in the full armor of God? Ask the Father to reveal to you where you are half dressed and how to remain suited.

Prayer prompt: Jesus, thank you for the victory that You won for me at Calvary! You won the ultimate victory, but I know that the devil continues to bring battles to me daily. I thank you Lord, that he is no match for You. So, Father, I pray now that You will help me to utilize the tools that You have given me to fight this spiritual battle. Help me to put on the full armor daily so that I may be fully dressed for battle. May I always be reminded that the war has already been won and I am more than a conqueror through Jesus Christ!

DAY 27: THE WORD OF GOD

"All scripture is given by inspiration of God, and is profitable for doctrine,
for reproof, for correction, for instruction in righteousness:"
2 Timothy 3:16 KJV

We discussed yesterday that the Word is a powerful weapon and is part of the armor that we should put on daily. Let's focus in a bit more closely on the Word of God and its importance. While there are definitely some interesting accounts in the Bible, the Word is more than a collection of Bible stories. It is a sharp and powerful two-edged sword. It will inspire, teach, and correct you. The Word will also penetrate and expose deception. As we saw yesterday, the Word is both a defensive and offensive weapon. It is an effective weapon to combat spiritual opposition when you are on assignment for the Lord and it is equally effective in provoking change in situations, atmospheres, and people.

Defensively, the Word can be used to pull down strongholds by countering the enemy's lies with truth and flooding dark places with light. We can use the Word to speak to strongholds and cause them to be dismantled. We are reminded of this truth in 2 Corinthians 10:4–5 (NKJV): *"For the weapons of our warfare are not carnal but mighty in God for pulling down strongholds, casting down arguments and every high thing that exalts itself against the knowledge of God, bringing every thought into captivity to the obedience of Christ."*

The Word is also an effective weapon when the enemy attacks with temptations. Jesus used the Word when the devil came to tempt him in the wilderness. When the devil attacked, Jesus didn't respond by engaging the devil in conversation or even trying to reason with him. He simply spoke the Word. Just as Jesus declared the Word to shut down the attacks of the enemy, we, too, can declare the Word to resist the devil's temptations. *"But he answered and said, It is written, Man shall not live by bread alone, but by every word that proceedeth out of the mouth of God" (Matt. 4:4 KJV).*

The Word of God is also an offensive weapon that can be used pre-emptively to aide us on our journey. When we speak the Word, we hear the spoken word and our faith is strengthened. Romans 10:17 (NKJV) reminds us that, *"faith comes by hearing, and hearing by the word of God."*

The Word of God shifts atmospheres and sets things in motion. In the beginning, we see God speaking creation into existence. Genesis details the account of the world being made by the Word of God. He said let there be, and it was. (Gen. 1) When we speak the Word of God in faith, we set things in motion in the spirit realm to cause things to come into alignment with what God has said. When you see areas in your life that don't align with the Word, begin to declare the Word of God over that area until it comes into alignment.

The Word will pinpoint the condition or your heart. The Word divides that which is good from that which is evil and reveals your true motivation and intentions. *"For the word of God is living and active, sharper than any two-edged sword, piercing to the division of soul and of spirit, of joints and of marrow, and discerning the thoughts and intentions of the heart" (Heb. 4:12 ESV).*

The Word is essential in the life of the believer and should not be regarded casually. Regular reading and studying of the Word must be a discipline that is loved and embraced to be effective on this kingdom journey. Jesus Himself is the Word. The evidence of the degree that we love the Lord is demonstrated by the love that we have for His Word.

Reflection: Make an assessment of your reading and study habits. Have you prioritized spending time in the Word? Take time to seek the Lord regarding how He would like to take you deeper in the Word. Make note of what the Lord reveals and commit to putting it into practice.

Prayer prompt: Thank you, Lord, that you have given me everything that I need in Your Word. Father, I ask that You create in me a greater hunger for You and Your Word. May I fall in love with Your Word all over again!

DAY 28: THE SECRET PLACE

"Now in the morning, having risen a long while before daylight,
He went out and departed to a solitary place; and there He prayed."
Mark 1:35 NKJV

The Bible tells us that Jesus regularly rose early in the morning to pray and spend time alone with the Father. Jesus understood that the pressures of this life would be great and that the only way to effectively manage and navigate our way through is by spending time with the Father and seeking His counsel. Jesus is our example of how we are to live this life. Demonstrating the importance of prayer, He regularly took time to enter the secret place with His Father.

When we look at Jesus' example of prayer, we see Him praying in the morning (Mark 1:35) and at night (Luke 6:12). We see Him going away to the secret place to pray after a long day of ministry (Matt. 14:23), as well as going to the secret place to pray before embarking on his final assignment at Calvary (Matt. 26:39). Jesus set the pattern that no matter the situation, we must make time to spend with the Father in prayer.

For us to manage and navigate life successfully, we, too, must commit to seeking God about everything. We must be purposeful and strategic in how we live our lives. Contrary to popular belief, the Father never intended us to wander aimlessly trying to figure out life. He longs to share His plans for our lives with us. He longs to give you insight and strategy. The Lord desires to spend time with each of us.

The secret place is a place of power. It is the place where we are strengthened, and it is the place where the Father can remind us of His truths. The secret place is where we come into agreement with the Father and war with the enemy. The secret place is also where the Father will hold us in His arms and comfort us when the cares of life weigh us down. When we enter the secret place of prayer with our Father, it is the place where we can come boldly with all our cares and concerns. It is the place where we can worship Him for being the loving Father that He is. It is the place where we can be transparent and honest without fear of judgement or shame. The secret place of prayer is where we grow in intimacy with the Father and learn to discern His voice and His will for our lives.

Let us not rush to start our day, only to run into a jam before we call on the Lord. Instead, let us become consistent in starting our day by seeking Him first. When we wake up, commit to spending time with Him, so that He can prepare you and equip you for that which you will run into on that day. As you continue throughout the day, talk with Him continually. Ask Him about the decisions and choices that you need to make. When things are confusing, ask Him to give you clarity. Pause to say thank you as you see Him move throughout your day. Take time to just tell Him that you love Him. And certainly be sure to make time to talk to Him before going to bed.

As you spend time in the secret place, understand that your prayers don't always have to be long. Just keep the conversation going. As you continue to do so, you will find that it will become more natural to talk to your Father, and you will desire to talk to Him more. The beautiful thing is that you will discover just how much He desires to talk to you too!

Reflection: How is your prayer life? Do you look to Him for strategy and direction, or do you find that you tend to talk to God about your decisions after they have been made? Make an assessment of your current prayer life. What areas of your prayer life can be strengthened?

Prayer Prompt: Thank you, Father, that I can come boldly to your throne of grace that I may obtain mercy and find grace to help in my time of need. Thank you for the invitation to talk to You and share my heart with You. I cannot be successful on this journey without You, and I desire to spend time with You even more in the place of prayer. I look forward to our time together to hear what You desire to say to me. I look to You for direction and counsel, and I thank you for Your wisdom, Your leading, and Your guidance.

Day 29: The Plan for Success

*"This Book of the Law shall not depart from your mouth,
but you shall meditate on it day and night, so that you may be
careful to do according to all that is written in it. For then you will
make your way prosperous, and then you will have good success."*
Joshua 1:8 ESV

After Moses died and the Lord commissioned Joshua to lead the children of Israel to the Promised Land, He gave Joshua the blueprint for success in his assignment. The secret wasn't long or complex. The Lord simply told Joshua to stay in the Word. Technically, the Lord told him to stay in the book of the law, which is the first five books of the Bible, as that was all that had been documented at that time. Nonetheless, the Lord was instructing Joshua to stick to what God had said. He told him to speak the Word, and He told Joshua to meditate on it continually.

The Lord told Joshua that speaking the Word and continual rehearsing of the Word through meditation was essential to his ability to do what the Word said. The degree to which Joshua would abide by the Word is the degree that he would experience success. His success was directly tied to him following what God had laid out in His Word.

The same is true for us today. To be effective and have true success in your assignment and in life is directly tied to doing things God's way. Just as the book of the law was the blueprint for Joshua's success, the Word of God is the blueprint for our success today. So, we, like Joshua, must spend time in the Word. We must meditate on and rehearse the Word continually. As we do, the Holy Spirit will cause the Word to dwell inside of us. He will write the Word on the tablets of our heart and even cause the Word to change the posture of our heart. As we speak the Word and declare it over our lives and situations, we will discover our faith rising to believe His Word. The more time that we spend in the Word, the more it becomes a part of our very nature and makeup. Our appetites and desires change, and we begin to want what God wants. As we consume the Word, our thinking changes and comes into greater alignment with God.

The Word of God is the guidebook that illuminates your steps and makes your path clear. If you want God's results, you must do it God's way. The blessing is that He doesn't hide His way from us. It's laid out in His Word. Just as the Lord told Joshua, when you remain in His Word and follow what it says, then success is guaranteed.

Reflection: What areas are you struggling to find success? Take time to search the Scripture to see what it says about the matter. Purpose to do as the Word instructs and watch the Lord bring His results.

Prayer prompt: Thank you, Lord, that You have given me the blueprint in Your Word for success. I recognize that there is no success apart from You. So, Father, I ask that You help me to treasure Your Word more than anything else so that I may prioritize spending time with You in Your Word. I thank you in advance for the transformative work that You will do in my life as I consume more and more of You.

Day 30: Deeper in Him

And ye shall seek me, and find me,
when ye shall search for me with all your heart.
Jeremiah 29:13 KJV

As we have journeyed through these past twenty-nine days, I'm sure you have begun to experience the Lord in greater ways. You have more resolve and genuinely believe that which He has placed in your heart can be achieved through Him. Now it's time to go even deeper. You must now go deeper in Him. Now is the time to intensify your prayer life. Now is the time to become more intentional in your study and devotion. Now is the time to sit before the Lord and allow Him to reveal even more about who He is and what He desires for your life.

The Lord has given you a glimpse, and He's placed a vision in your heart. You will find, however, as you become more intentional in seeking Him, He will begin to reveal the steps that He will have you to take. Not only will He reveal your next steps toward fulfilling the promise, but He will also begin to show you the things inside of you that are a hindrance to your forward progress. He will show you what's in you that looks like Him as well as that which is in you that doesn't look like Him. You may find that He begins to ask you to separate from some people or things that are impeding intimacy with Him. As you go deeper, it will be during your intimate time with Him that He will begin revealing even more of His heart to you as it pertains to your life.

Though you may be tempted to forge ahead in your new level of resolve, make it a priority to go to a new level of intimacy with the Father. Recognize that this journey is not a sprint, but a marathon. There is so much more that the Father desires to reveal to you. What you have seen thus far is not all there is to see. He is an infinite God, so you will never come to the end of who He is.

As you continue to seek Him and earnestly desire more of Him and His will for your life, He will begin to reveal Himself to you even the more. As He reveals more of Himself, He will also give you a greater understanding of who you are in Him and the purpose that He has for your life. You will gain greater understanding and clarity regarding why you had to experience the things that you did in life. He will also show you how He desires to use those experiences for His glory! Go deeper. He has so much more in store for you.

Reflection: As you purpose to go deeper in the Lord, be intentional about making time to spend with Him daily. As you pray, make time to also just sit with Him and listen for what He desires to say. Keep a journal or something to take note of what the Lord says to you in your time together. Talk to Him as you would a friend. As a part of your time with the Lord, consume the Word. He is His Word. Take your time as you read and study. Meditate on His Word. Allow the Word to penetrate your heart. Ask the Father questions about what you read and expect Him to give you answers and greater revelation about Himself.

Prayer prompt: Thank you, Father, for this journey and all that You have allowed me to experience thus far. I acknowledge that what I have experienced of You is not all that there is to experience and so, Lord, I want to go deeper in You. Father, I submit myself to you.

Holy Spirit, guide me and lead me as I intentionally set my heart on knowing You more. I love you, Lord, and wherever You lead, I am willing to follow.

Day 31: Wait on the Lord

"But they that wait upon the Lord shall renew their strength;
they shall mount up with wings as eagles; they shall run,
and not be weary; and they shall walk, and not faint."
Isaiah 40:31 KJV

Many times, when God gives us an assignment, we start off patiently listening to the voice of God. We listen as we get the details on what it is that the Lord is asking us to do. But, too often, as we start moving forward and working to bring the vision to pass, we find that we are no longer walking with God but instead have rushed ahead of God. When this happens, we usually don't notice it at first, but after a while, we find ourselves tired and burnt out. We may start asking God why He even has us doing this. The work may begin to seem futile, and we may begin to wonder, what's the point? If we aren't careful, we may even find ourselves in a place where we are ready to throw up our hands and walk completely away from the assignment that we have been given.

Oh, how easy it is to drift from patiently waiting on the Lord. I know because I am unfortunately guilty of finding myself in that place more times than I care to admit. But I have learned that when we begin to truly wait on the Lord, He will supply us with all that we need to perform that which He has purposed for us to do in life. Our focus verse of the day reiterates this same principle.

When we look at the verse, we see that it begins with the word "but" which indicates what follows is a contrast to what was stated

previously. So, let us also look at the preceding verse. When we examine verse 30, we see that it is talking about how even those who
are young and full of vitality will eventually become tired and ex-
hausted when they are operating in their own strength. This lets us
know that as people, we have a limited capacity and there is only
so much that we can do on our own. However, verse 31 tells us that
when we wait on the Lord, when we move at His pace, He continually renews our strength such that we have the capacity to continue
to go without becoming weary or fainting.

Waiting on the Lord causes us to move in a rhythm that is not determined by us, but rather one that is determined by Him alone. Waiting
on the Lord requires a surrender of our agenda in exchange for His.
When we wait on the Lord, we wait with expectation and with the
knowledge and understanding that we are totally reliant on Him for
strength to endure the journey. When we wait on the Lord, we expect
Him to enable us to do all that He asks, and we acknowledge that our
ability is solely dependent on Him working through us.

Reflection: Do you find waiting challenging? What do find the most
challenging about the waiting process? Pray and ask the Lord to
teach you to wait patiently on Him.

Prayer prompt: Dear Father, thank you for Your divine timing. Thank
you, Lord, that You have the times and seasons all mapped out. Teach
me to move in concert with You. Teach me how to wait on You. And
as I wait, may I always wait with earnest expectation, knowing that
You will supply all that I need for this journey.

Day 32: A Time for Everything

"To every thing there is a season,
and a time to every purpose under the heaven:"
Ecclesiastes 3:1 KJV

From the beginning of time, God has ordained and orchestrated everything that happens and the timing in which it is to happen. God's timing is perfect. We can be sure that which God has ordained shall come to pass in its proper season.

But even knowing this, if we are honest, sometimes it can seem difficult to wait on God's timing. As you continue to pray that the Lord gives you strength to wait on Him, also know that time is never wasted or meaningless to God. Every minute of every day is intentional with Him.

As much as we may have moments that we desire to rush God, we must never forget that time is also a tool that God uses to develop us. He uses seasons in our lives to mature us and grow us. God has already assigned an appointed time for every season that you will go through. In His wisdom, He knows what it will take and even how long it will take for you to grow and get all that He desires to pour into you in that season. In His omniscience, He even accounts for those times when we choose to exercise our free will and move contrary to His perfect will for our lives. He wastes nothing. Even the plans orchestrated by the devil that were meant for evil, God uses them for our good.

In the natural, we all know that fruit takes time to grow and ripen before its natural richness and sweetness can be enjoyed. Throughout the Bible, the Lord declares that believers should bear fruit. In fact, in John 15:8, we see that when believers bear fruit; the Father is glorified, and we prove that we are His disciples. This fruit we bear as believers is spiritual fruit that others who will connect and cross your path can consume and benefit from. Just as natural fruit takes time to mature, so does spiritual fruit. Fruit picked before time is bitter. It's not appetizing or satisfying to the one consuming it. As a matter of fact, if the fruit is not ripe enough, it may actually make the one eating it sick instead of providing the intended nourishment.

In this season of waiting, God is developing you. Submit to the process that He is taking you through and allow Him to perfect that which He is doing in your life in this season. The beautiful thing about seasons is that seasons change. They don't last forever. Go through this season with patience and expectation, knowing that He is producing something beautiful in you. Know that your fruit is ripening and at the appointed time He will bring you out, and all those He has ordained to eat from your tree will reap the full benefit of that which He has done in your life.

Reflection: Ask the Father to place a desire in you to receive the fullness of all that He desires to complete in your life in this season and every season to come. Ask Him to cause you to desire His perfect will over quick and temporary satisfaction. Pray that you will submit to the Father's timing in areas of your life so that the fruit from your life will be at its best for all those He has assigned to eat from your tree.

Prayer prompt: Thank you, Lord, for this season of my life. Thank you, Father, for perfecting everything that concerns me. In this season, as I wait on You, I submit to Your perfecting process. Have Your perfect will in my life.

DAY 33: A PURE HEART

"Search me, O God, and know my heart: try me,
and know my thoughts: And see if there be any wicked way in me,
and lead me in the way everlasting."
Psalm 139:23–24 KJV

Our Father is not like man, judging from the exterior. No, He looks at the condition of our heart. The Lord discerns the motives and intents of our heart. He knows the "why" behind every action that we take. It is imperative that we continually do a heart check to ensure the motive and reasoning behind why we do what we do is from a pure place.

The Lord wants to bless you. He desires to prosper you and bring your dreams to pass. While all of this is true, more than anything, He desires that our heart align with His. He doesn't want the motivation behind what we do to be for selfish gain or to bring glory to ourselves. His desire is that all we do be done out of love with a sincere desire to see others edified and the Father glorified.

Does this mean that it is wrong to desire to be successful? Absolutely not! God desires for His children to be successful and prosper. All throughout the Old Testament, we see where the Lord worked on behalf of His people to bring them success in their God-given endeavors. He allowed His people to defeat nations greater than themselves. He positioned His people to have favor and influence. He even caused His people to have wealth and material goods. God has no issue with His children prospering. He simply desires that we want to please Him more than we desire to prosper.

Matthew 6:21 (KJV) says, *"For where your treasure is, there will your heart be also."* The things that we treasure will be the things that we hold to most tightly. The things we treasure will also be the things that we pursue most aggressively. What is it that you treasure? What is it that consumes your heart and, as a result, your time, your energy, and your money?

In our focus verse, David recognized that the only One who sees our heart clearly and can discern our true motives is the Lord. So, he cried out to the Lord to search his heart and examine his thought life to see if they were in alignment with God. We, too, must be like David and submit our heart and thoughts to the all-seeing eyes of our Heavenly Father, that He may reveal to us our true motives and everything in us that does not align with Him.

Reflection: Invite the Father to search your heart and to check your motives. Ask Him to reveal what is in your heart. If there be any unclean or impure thing in there, repent and ask for forgiveness. Then ask the Lord to align your heart with His. Ask Him to make His desire for your life your desire. And as your desires begin to come into alignment with His desires, watch Him open doors to bring them to pass.

Prayer prompt: Echoing David's prayer, search me, O God, and know my heart. Try me and know my thoughts. See if there is any wicked way in me and lead me in the way everlasting. Father, I repent for every impure motive and unclean thought. Create in me a clean heart, O God, and renew a right spirit within me. Thank you, Father, for transforming my heart, such that my heart comes into alignment with Yours.

DAY 34: STAY FOCUSED

"But when he saw the wind boisterous, he was afraid;
and beginning to sink, he cried, saying, Lord, save me.
And immediately Jesus stretched forth his hand, and caught him,
and said unto him, O thou of little faith, wherefore didst thou doubt?"
Matthew 14:30–31 KJV

We started this journey recounting how God bid Peter to come, and Peter got out of the ship at the word of God. He exercised his faith and stepped out on that which God spoke. The Bible says, not only did he step out, but that Peter actually walked on water. He defied the laws of gravity and what was known to be possible and did the impossible.

But something happened as Peter walked on the water. He took his eyes off Jesus and began to notice the wind. Both Mark and John's account of this story indicate that the wind was blowing fiercely even before Peter got out of the ship. However, even though the storm was brewing and the wind was blowing, Peter's initial focus was so fastened on Jesus that he was oblivious to his circumstances. However, when Peter took his eyes off Jesus, he got distracted by his circumstances. He noticed the winds and the storm. Peter lost his focus and became afraid.

Can you relate to Peter? God tells you to do a thing and you finally work up the courage to start. At first, you are excited because you are finally taking that step of faith. All seems well, but then you run into an obstacle. Something happens and you begin to see all that could go wrong. What initially seemed like a good idea suddenly seems all wrong. Fear and doubt set in and you begin to look for the quickest way of escape. You look for a retreat to the safety and comfort of your "boat." Have you ever been there?

As you are on this journey pursuing that which you are called to do, know that there will be circumstances and situations strategically placed by the enemy to distract and discourage you. You must learn to stay focused and keep your eyes, mind, and your heart on the word that you heard from the Lord. For when you lose your focus, you are more susceptible to having your faith challenged by the distractions around you. Remember, there was no difference in the waves and the blowing wind from when Peter stepped off the ship to the time that he began to sink. The only thing that changed was Peter's focus. Stay focused!

Reflection: Ask the Lord to continue to help to maintain your focus on Him during this journey. Identify things that you can do to help you keep your eyes focused on Jesus.

Prayer prompt: Dear Lord, I know distractions will come to try to discourage me and hinder me from that which You have assigned my hands to do. Help me to keep my eyes focused on You!

DAY 35: STEADFAST AND UNMOVABLE

"Therefore, my beloved brethren, be ye stedfast, unmoveable,
always abounding in the work of the Lord, forasmuch as ye know
that your labour is not in vain in the Lord."
1 Corinthians 15:58 KJV

The beautiful thing about being a child of God is that He never asks us to figure out the path or figure out how to do life. He simply instructs us to follow Him. We are following the One who is the Alpha and the Omega, the beginning and the end. The One who created all and was here before time began. Our Father is Jehovah, I AM That I AM, the self-existent God. No one created Him. No one counsels Him. He is omniscient and all wise. There is nothing that escapes His knowledge. Not even the plans for your life. He knows everything. He is omnipresent. He is everywhere at the same time. He is wherever you are and wherever you need Him to be. He is all seeing. He is God and never slumbers nor sleeps. Nothing gets past His all-seeing eyes. He sees it all. He has seen every moment and detail of your past, your present and your future. What an Awesome God! What's even more awesome is that we who have accepted Jesus as Savior also have the privilege of calling Him Father!

The truth is, though, sometimes we have to remind ourselves of who our Father is because when we do, it also reminds us of His ability. Recalling who is leading us helps to give us assurance that no matter what we encounter on this journey, we will make it to the destination. We are walking step by step and day by day, but our Father has already seen the end. He knows how everything will work together. So, as you continue forward, be encouraged to know that when you keep your hand in the Father's hand that you will see the fruit of your labor.

When it's not working out the way you expected or as fast as you expected, don't waiver. Stay the course. Continue in the work and the assignment that the Father has given you. We've already talked about the haters, so you know they will come. Suit up daily. Set your mind on the assignment before you and be resolved that no matter what happens that you will not waiver from the task. Slow down when needed, but do not quit. Take joy in knowing the assignment is bigger than you and that the Lord has selected you to partner with Him for the work that He desires to see on the earth. Your assignment matters. The fruit may not be visible yet, but it will manifest at the appointed time, and someone's life will be enriched because of the work that you are doing.

So, I leave you with the words of apostle Paul in 1 Corinthians 15:58, in the NIV translation, *"Therefore, my dear brothers and sisters, stand firm. Let nothing move you. Always give yourselves fully to the work of the Lord, because you know that your labor in the Lord is not in vain."*

Reflection: What are you facing currently that has brought discouragement in your assignment? What has been the impact of the discouragement? Has it caused you to slow down or threatened to cause you to step away from your assignment? Take a moment and reflect on your current challenges and their impacts on your forward progress. Make note of any areas that your commitment or determination has waivered. As you reflect on today's focus verse, submit every area of discouragement to the Father in prayer as you seek His strength to remain unmovable.

Prayer prompt: Thank you, Lord, that you were here at the beginning of time and You shall be here at the end. Thank you, Lord, that even in the present moment, You are here, and You know exactly how this assignment will fit into Your greater plan. Lord, help me to always remember that the assignment is not just about me, but about Your kingdom. Father I present every area of discouragement and frustration pertaining to this assignment to you. Help me to be steadfast and unmovable so that I don't abandon the assignment. Thank you, Lord, that nothing is wasted in You, so I trust You with my life and with what You have assigned my hands to do.

DAY 36: PRESS...

"I press toward the mark for the prize of the
high calling of God in Christ Jesus."
Philippians 3:14 KJV

One of the wonderful things about the Bible is that we are able to see and learn from the examples of those who have walked before us. The apostle Paul is one such person whose life is filled with examples for us to glean from as he faithfully moved in his God-given assignment.

In the third chapter of Philippians, we see that Paul is encouraging believers to press toward the goal. He even goes as far as declaring that his goal is *"to know Christ and experience the mighty power that raised him from the dead."* He goes on to say that he wants to *"suffer with him, sharing in his death."* (Phil. 3:10 NLT) Paul has realized that all the things he used to think held value are really worthless and his one true goal is to know Christ. He acknowledges that while this is his goal, he hasn't yet arrived at that place, but he's still aiming for it.

Further in the chapter, Paul recognizes the power distractions can have to hinder reaching the objective, so he declares that he is focused. Not only is he not looking at what is occurring around him now, he says that he is forgetting what has happened in the past (v. 13). He's determined not to let current challenges, nor the memory of past successes or failures, deter him from obtaining his goal.

After all of this, he says, "I press" (v. 14). The word press means to apply pressure. We can use the word in many contexts but whether we are pressing the elevator button or pressing a shirt, what remains true is that to press involves two elements coming together such that one applies pressure on the other to cause movement or a change in its current state. When Paul declares, "I press," he acknowledges that he is the one who will apply pressure. He is making it known that he will apply pressure to whatever forces that stand between him and his goal until they are moved out of his way. Paul is not waiting for someone else to do it. He recognizes that there is effort that he must put into achieving the goal. He declares that he has a target in mind, and he is resolved not to let anything get in his way.

This is the level of determination that you must have towards seeing the fulfillment of the assignment that God has given you. Paul knew that the fulfillment of his goal would result in him receiving the prize of coming to know Jesus even more. What is the prize that you are looking forward to receiving at the completion of your goal? I encourage you today to take a page out of the apostle Paul's book and press! Press through the setbacks and press through the heartache. Press when you are motivated and press even more when you are not. Press through everything that tries to keep you from obtaining your goal! Make this your declaration, "I PRESS!"

Reflection: What things are currently challenging you as you work toward your goal? How is your press? Take a moment to assess the degree to which you are pressing toward your goal. Seek the Lord for strategy and wisdom to press past the current challenge. Make up your mind that you will press! Let nothing stand in the way of you getting to the finish line.

Prayer prompt: Thank you, Lord, for the example of apostle Paul and his life's work of ministry. Thank you for the example of fortitude and resolve to press toward the goal. Father, help me to press. Help me to continue to press forward in every season that I may see the assignment completed.

Day 37: Such a Time as This

"For if thou altogether holdest thy peace at this time, then shall there enlargement and deliverance arise to the Jews from another place; but thou and thy father's house shall be destroyed: and who knoweth whether thou art come to the kingdom for such a time as this?"
Esther 4:14 KJV

The book of Esther tells the story of a young girl named Hadassah. When her mother and father died, her cousin Mordecai took her in and raised her as his daughter. Hadassah, also known as Esther, was a beautiful and lovely young lady. However, she and her cousin Mordecai were descendants of the Jews who had been carried away in captivity to Babylon by King Nebuchadnezzar and were subject to a life of servanthood.

One day the King made a proclamation that all the young virgins in the province were to be brought to him so that he could find the next queen. Esther was amongst those brought to the King. As the Lord would have it, she found favor in the King's sight and was selected to be the queen. A girl who didn't fit the mold and by tradition was highly unlikely to become queen, did just that. This lets us know that it's not our background or pedigree that man may require that determines our qualification, but rather it's the Lord who does the selection, and whom the Lord selects, he qualifies.

But we must also know that when the Lord selects us, He also has a purpose for us. Never forget that every God-given assignment has a God-given purpose attached to it. As was the case with Esther. While

Esther was promoted to the palace, the King had a top official who was plotting the destruction of Mordecai and his Jewish kinsmen. Mordecai sent word to Esther of the plot and told her to go to the King on their behalf. Although Esther was queen, she also knew that there was a law that anyone who went before the King uninvited was subject to be put to death, unless he extended his golden scepter. When Esther shared this with Mordecai, he reminded her that if she chose to be fearful and not take the assignment, then someone else would be raised up to accomplish God's plan. But he also left her with some food for thought—perhaps this is the reason that you are in the position that you are in; so that you can be the one to complete the assignment.

There is nothing coincidental with God. He is intentional in every-thing that He does. When He places you in position and gives you an assignment, He has a purpose that He has destined you to ful-fill. In Esther's case, God positioned her to have favor with the King so that the lives of the Jews would be spared. God has positioned you and given you an assignment that has purpose attached to it as well. Esther could have passed on the assignment and kept silent. As Mordecai reminded her, if she had chosen that route, many lives would have been at stake.

You may not know the lives attached to the assignment that God has given you, but it is safe to say that God has purposed it to make an impact in someone's life. Never discount the impact of your yes. Just as the yes of an orphan turned queen saved a nation, who knows the significance your assignment will make in the lives of others. You have been selected and positioned for a time such as this.

Reflection: God uses regular people to do extraordinary things. Often when we look at the things that God assigns us to do, we underestimate the impact of our yes. Usually, the purpose of the assignment is far greater than what we imagine or think. The thing is that only God knows the ultimate purpose for His ask. Your part is to be a willing vessel that He can use.

Prayer prompt: Lord, I don't know all of what You have planned, but I give You a yes all over again. I thank you for walking with me and choosing to use me as a vessel that You can work through.

_____

_____

_____

_____

_____

_____

_____

_____

_____

_____

_____

_____

_____

_____

_____

_____

_____

_____

_____

_____

_____

_____

_____

_____

_____

DAY 38: YOU WERE BUILT FOR THIS

"For we are his workmanship, created in Christ Jesus for good works,
which God prepared beforehand, that we should walk in them."
Ephesians 2:10 ESV

When we accepted Jesus as Savior, we were saved from the penalty of sin. We were saved by grace not as a result of anything that we did. It is not because of how good or faithful we are that dictates our salvation. Salvation is a free gift given as a result of our belief and confession that Jesus is Lord. When we accepted Jesus as Savior, Ephesians tells us that the Lord created us anew in Christ Jesus. Verse 10 tells us that we are God's workmanship. Other translations say we are his masterpiece. Both workmanship and masterpiece convey the fact that we are incredibly special to God. It lets us know that God took his time and fashioned and formed us. He put thought and consideration into everything that concerns us. But most importantly, it lets us know that when He finished with us, He was pleased with His creation. Beloved, God is pleased with you! He called you His workmanship, His masterpiece!

It's important to note that He didn't take His time fashioning and forming us for no reason. He was so specific and intentional about us because we were created for a specific purpose that God predetermined from the beginning of time. The great news is that when we accepted Jesus as Savior, we became new creatures who are now equipped to go forth and fulfill the purpose that He designed for us to fulfill from the beginning of time.

Before accepting Jesus, we went about life according to our own plans. We did what we wanted to do according to what we thought was right. More importantly, before salvation, we operated in our own strength and ability. A strength and ability which is limited. However, at the time of salvation, the Holy Spirit takes up residence in us. We receive supernatural help to equip us to do all that God designed for us to do. So often, the struggles that we experience in life are simply because we are trying to navigate life without seeking God's help. When we fail to seek Him for direction, we often find ourselves in places that He never intended us to be. When we try to operate in our own strength, we find ourselves tired, worn out, and frustrated.

God never intended you and me to fulfill our life's purpose outside of Him. It is His desire that we allow Him to work through us to fulfill the plans that He has for us. This assignment that He has you on now didn't take Him by surprise. He's put everything in you that you will need to fulfill it. He's just waiting for you to walk in it with Him.

Reflection: Consider what it is that the Lord has assigned you to do. Now reflect on the fact that He created you specifically to accomplish this and other good works. Think about the fact that your Father has equipped you with everything that you would need to successfully be able to do what He assigns your hands to do. How does this knowledge shape your actions moving forward?

Prayer prompt: Father, thank you for creating me for a specific purpose. Father, may I always be reminded that You have already laid the path for me to walk in with You.

DAY 39: WALK IN YOUR AUTHORITY

*"Behold, I have given you authority to tread on serpents and scorpions,
and over all the power of the enemy, and nothing shall hurt you."*
Luke 10:19 ESV

As children of God, there are certain privileges that we have that others do not have. One such privilege is authority over the forces of darkness. Consider our focus verse. Jesus told his disciples that He gave them authority over all the power of the enemy. This same power that Jesus gave to His followers back then is the same power that Jesus has given to us as believers today.

The text says believers have authority, and the enemy has power. Let's look at those words a little closer. Power denotes strength and ability. However, authority goes a step further, and it means to have the legal right to use the power given to you to rule or enforce. Notice that Jesus gave believers authority over the enemy's power. Side note: There is a false theology floating around that says the enemy doesn't have any power. The text is clear that it is not true. Don't let people fool you with that false theology and lull you into a place of complacency, thinking that the enemy doesn't have any power. The enemy does have power. More importantly, the Lord has given us authority over the enemy's power.

This means that as children of God, we don't have to sit around and be the devil's punching bag. We don't have to idly watch on the sidelines as he wreaks havoc in our lives. No, we have been authorized by heaven. We can take authority over his plots and plans.

This means that when we see the enemy at work, it's time for us to use our authority to decree, declare, and dismantle the plans of darkness in Jesus' mighty name. Our authority comes from the One who lives inside of us. The Holy Spirit lives inside of us and He is greater than anyone that will come up against us. As a matter of fact, 1 John 4:4b (KJV) reminds us that *"greater is he that is in you, than he that is in the world."*

As you boldly move forward, continue in prayer about everything. When you sense the enemy's hand at work causing confusion, chaos, or delay, take authority over the work of the enemy. Open your mouth and declare what God has said. Use the Word. Remember that the world was framed by the word of God. The Word shifts atmospheres and disrupts demonic plots. God has given you an assignment. Accept nothing less than His results for the assignment. If God said it, say what He has said until you see it! Continue in communication with Him every step of the way. Live righteously and He will guide your path. (Ps. 37:23)

Reflection: What area is the enemy wreaking havoc in your life? What have you been putting up with that you need to take authority over? Search Scriptures as it pertains to those areas. Stand up in your God-given authority. As you follow the leading of the Holy Spirit, make declarations in faith according to what God has said over those areas.

Prayer prompt: Thank you, Lord, for granting me Your authority over the power of the enemy. Father, I repent for any way that I have come into agreement with the enemy as it pertains to my life. Today, I stand in the authority that You have given me, and I declare that no weapons formed against me shall prosper, in Jesus' name.

DAY 40: WALK BY FAITH

"For we walk by faith, not by sight:"
2 Corinthians 5:7 KJV

Over these last thirty-nine days, God has spoken to you and ministered to you in various ways. For some, the Lord has caused you to walk into a greater revelation of who He is in your life. For others, He has opened your eyes to who you are in Him. Regardless of which category you find yourself in today, know that the Lord is not done. He has only just begun.

He desires to continue this wonderful journey with you as He helps you fulfill the very thing that He placed in your heart to do. As you continue in the faith walk with the Lord, remember that we don't rely on what we see, because what we see can be deceptive. Often, what we see with our natural eye is not truly as it seems or even what it shall be. This is why we are reminded as believers that we walk by faith and not by sight. In other words, we are to walk solely based on what the Lord has said.

We can't allow our circumstances or surroundings to dictate our actions, but we must rely on the Father to dictate our every move. He placed the dream in our heart. He is the One that will bring fulfillment, so we can trust that He also knows the path we should take.

So, as you prepare to continue moving forward, remember that nothing is impossible with God. Since He called you to this assignment,

He will supply all the needed provisions. Keep your ear to His mouth and continue to trust Him as you Walk on the Word!

Reflection: When we walk by sight, we are dependent on our own ability to discern and make decisions. However, when we walk by faith, we surrender the situation to God and we declare that we trust His direction, His leading, and His Word about the matter. Pray and ask the Lord to reveal any areas in which you have been moving according to your own sight line. As the Lord reveals, pray and ask the Lord what He has to say about those areas. Ask Him to increase your faith so that you surrender control over the outcome and truly walk by faith.

Prayer prompt: Thank you, Lord, for walking with me over these last forty days. I am determined to walk by faith into the fulfillment of what You have planned for me. Lord, I ask that You show me the areas in which I am still trying to hold on and control. Help me to grow in my faith walk so that I trust You even more with every area of my life. I love you, Lord, and I thank you!

Prayer of Salvation

"For God so loved the world, that he gave his only begotten Son,
that whosoever believeth in him should not perish,
but have everlasting life.
John 3:16 KJV

These last forty days have been powerful, but I do not take for granted that everyone has a personal relationship with Jesus Christ. The Lord loves you. Not a perfect version of you, but He loves you for who you are right now. He sees you and cares about everything that concerns you. He knows all about you. He knows all your sins and still loves you so much that He is inviting you into a relationship with Him today. More importantly, God loves you so much that He sent His Son, Jesus, to earth so that we could have a relationship and live eternally with Him. Jesus took on the sins of the world and willingly gave His life so that everyone who accepts Him as Savior will be saved from eternal damnation.

Have you accepted Jesus in your heart as Savior? If not, you can be saved today. There is nothing you can do to work or earn salvation. Salvation is a free gift given to all who confess Jesus is Lord and believes God raised Him from the dead. Romans 10:9-10 (NKJV) tells us, *"that if you confess with your mouth the Lord Jesus and believe in your heart that God has raised Him from the dead, you will be saved. For with the heart one believes unto righteousness, and with the mouth confession is made unto salvation."* Your faith in Jesus is the key to your salvation. Will you make a choice to accept Jesus as Savior?

If you desire to be saved today, pray this in faith:

> God, I confess that I am a sinner in need of a Savior. I have done things that are not pleasing to You, and I ask for Your forgiveness. I thank You for Your great love. I believe that Jesus is the only begotten Son of God and He is Lord. I believe that He died and rose again from the grave. I invite Jesus into my life today and accept Him as my Savior. In Jesus' name. Amen.

If you prayed this in faith, you are now saved! Your faith in Jesus assures your salvation. As a next step, it is important to connect with a Bible teaching, Bible believing ministry that will disciple you and help you grow stronger in the Lord. I am excited about your decision to accept Jesus as Savior. Welcome to the family of God!

ABOUT ERELETHEIA ALLEN

Ereletheia Allen is a licensed and ordained minister of the gospel of Jesus Christ. She is a Jesus lover, and she makes no qualms about it! Ereletheia is a profound preacher, teacher, and prophetic voice for this current dispensation. She is an ardent prayer warrior and has seen firsthand the miraculous work God has done in response to prayer. She serves as an associate minister at New Home Baptist Church under the leadership of Pastor Anthony R. Medlock. Ereletheia is also the servant leader of the Healing and Deliverance Ministry at New Home.

Ereletheia was saved at an early age, but it would be decades later before she truly understood just how much her heavenly Father loved her. This revelation changed her life forever and sparked an even greater passion to see others embrace the love of God for themselves and walk in the liberty that Christ died for us to have. It is Ereletheia's sincere desire to see people around the world saved, healed, delivered, and set free from the chains and bondage that hold them bound. It is her heart's desire that all know Jesus and have their own intimate relationship with Him. As she looks at the world today, she sees that so many are blinded by the schemes of satan, both inside and outside of the church. She aims to be a vessel used by the Lord to dispel satan's lies through the proclamation of the Gospel of Jesus Christ by way of the preached and taught Word.

Ereletheia is a certified Biblical Life Coach and lay-counselor. She is the founder and CEO of Focused on Your Future International, LLC, through which she does teaching and coaching to equip the body of Christ to live life victoriously. Ereletheia is also the President and Founder of Focused on Your Future Christian Life Ministries, Inc., (FoYFCLM) a 501c3 nonprofit organization aimed at ministering to the physical and spiritual needs of women. It is through FoYFCLM that she founded the I AM Who God Says I AM Movement aimed to help people around the world come to know, embrace, and walk in their unique God-given identity. When she is asked about her mission in life, her response is simple, "To live life fully surrendered to the Father!"

Out of all the titles that Ereletheia wears, her favorite titles are that of wife, mother, and GiGi. Rev. Allen resides in Bowie, Maryland and is happily married to the love of her life, Kenneth. They are the parents of four adult children and grandparents to five beautiful grandchildren: Kynnedy, Bryce, Avery, Kayden, and Ariya.

Connect and Share

Thank you for reading *Walking on the Word*. If you enjoyed this book, please leave a review on Amazon and the website where you purchased it.

Connect with the author on Facebook: Ereletheia Allen and Instagram @ereletheia. Visit her online at foyfinternational.com.

www.ingramcontent.com/pod-product-compliance
Lightning Source LLC
Chambersburg PA
CBHW071300130626
46556CB00003B/1397